D1012388

"In their book, Jean Gatz and Connie ... high-performance behaviors that top cor... ing for. Jean and Connie have combined i... ... ... scenarios, and practical advice into a clear, concise blueprint that will help professionals bring value to their jobs and enhance their performance for their teams."

Kim Wallenhorst, NCR Corporation Director,
HR Community Development

"After thirty years in business, I can assure you this is a clear, practical, and compelling guide to the elements of successful career building in an incredibly competitive employment market . . . definitely a career survival kit that will take you into the 21st century."

Robert C. Cochran, Senior Vice President,
NationsBank (ret.)

"If an employee adheres to the 'rules of success' outlined in Jean Gatz and Connie Podesta's book, they should be able to obtain job security with eventual advancement. *How to Be the Person Successful Companies Fight to Keep* should be read by everyone entering their professional life, as well as others seeking to brush up on their work skills. This book is destined to become a business classic and is one I highly recommend to my employees."

Art Favre, President,
Performance Contractors, Inc.

"An eye-opening and insightful guide to advancing your career. Connie Podesta and Jean Gatz creatively combine real-life scenarios, extensive research, and invaluable advice into this practical, easy-to-read book."

David Hayes, CEO,
Tempus Software, Inc.

"A readable and extremely valuable guide for both managers and employees. In a very concise way, Connie Podesta and Jean Gatz have built a framework for personal and corporate success. Strongly recommended!"

Gary R. Garcia, Field Executive,
Royal Insurance

"Employees who incorporate the behaviors described in this book into their professional and personal life will definitely add value to their employer and stay in demand in today's highly competitive global job market. This book should be required reading for everyone interested in his or her own job security."

**J. Sheldon Fortenberry, Manager of Engineering,
Chevron Petroleum Technology Co.**

"Companies are constantly looking for those employees who add value to their jobs by contributing to their profitability, success, and growth. Take responsibility for your professional life and read Podesta and Gatz's book, which is packed with current CEO and workplace expectations—time and money well spent! Required reading for the successful professional."

**Roger Heck, Executive Director,
Strasburger & Price, L.L.P.**

"As a human resources professional, I constantly see people drifting from one job to another, letting others determine where and for how long they will continue to work. In *How to Be the Person Successful Companies Fight to Keep,* Jean Gatz and Connie Podesta have provided a remarkable resource for creating your own job security by taking charge of your professional life and transforming careers when necessary. It applies to both private and public sector personnel."

**Esther Coleman, Executive Director,
American Association of Personnel Directors**

"In our business, employee turnover runs high. By incorporating the down-to-earth approach in *How to Be the Person Successful Companies Fight to Keep,* I feel confident we can drastically reduce our turnover rate. Every CEO, manager, and employee needs to read this book . . . and take notes!"

**Gary Kirlin, President,
Kirlin's Hallmark**

"Successful companies and managers who want to win and keep loyal and satisfied customers should buy a copy of this book for every employee and make it required reading. Employees who follow the advice will help build a company their customers will fight to keep."

Michael LeBoeuf,
author of *The Perfect Business* and
How to Win Customers and Keep Them for Life

"Downsized, merged, or restructured? If those all-too-common phrases describe your career, you're probably also well acquainted with their partners: stress, sleeplessness, and fear. This refreshingly honest book shows you how to take charge of your career and create your own job security."

Mike Johnson, General Manager, Division Operations,
Montana Power Co.

"A phenomenal book! This is like having the nation's most successful CEOs as my personal career counselors. The authors have condensed extensive research among CEOs, managers, human resource directors, and supervisors into a powerful, reader-friendly book that will help professionals remain marketable."

David Treen, Former U.S. Congressman and Governor,
State of Louisiana

"Much, much more than two authors' opinions . . . this book is packed with current workplace survey responses. Every CEO of every successful company will want each and every employee to have a copy of this 'must read' handbook."

William J. Doré, President & CEO,
Global Industries, Ltd.

F

How to Be the Person Successful Companies Fight to Keep

THE INSIDER'S GUIDE TO BEING NUMBER ONE IN THE WORKPLACE

Connie Podesta and Jean Gatz

A FIRESIDE BOOK
PUBLISHED BY SIMON & SCHUSTER

FIRESIDE
Rockefeller Center
1230 Avenue of the Americas
New York, NY 10020

Copyright © 1997 by Connie Podesta and Jean Gatz
All rights reserved, including the right of reproduction
in whole or in part in any form.

First Fireside Edition 1998

FIRESIDE and colophon are registered trademarks
of Simon & Schuster Inc.

Designed by Irving Perkins Associates

Manufactured in the United States of America

10

The Library of Congress has cataloged the Simon & Schuster
edition as follows:
Podesta, Connie.
   How to be the person successful companies fight to keep : the
   insider's guide to being number one in the workplace / Connie
   Podesta and Jean Gatz.
      p. cm.
      includes index.
      1. Success in business. 2. Performance. 3. Self-realization.
   4. Career development. I. Gatz, Jean. II. Title.
   HF5386.P748 1997   96-52718
   650.1—dc21   CIP

ISBN-13: 978-0-684-83032-2
ISBN-10: 0-684-83032-9
ISBN-13: 978-0-684-84008-6 (Pbk)
ISBN-10: 0-684-84008-1 (Pbk)

Contents

Introduction: There Are No Guarantees

Every day in this country, between two thousand and three thousand people lose their jobs. We've all heard the *official* words companies use to describe the process: *redesigning, right-sizing, restructuring, downsizing,* and *reengineering.* You may even have heard some of the more creative descriptions: *career change opportunity, decruitment, degrowing, dehiring, destaffing, personnel surplus reduction, redeployment,* and *redirectment.* Some of our favorites are: *redundancy elimination, skill mix adjustment,* and *workforce imbalance correction.* However sophisticated (or ridiculous) these terms are, there is no way to soften the blow of what they really mean: *eliminated, let go, laid off,* and *fired.*

Most of us know someone—a family member, friend, neighbor, or associate—who has lost a job. According to a recent *New York Times* analysis of Labor Department numbers, more than 43 million jobs have been eliminated in the United States since 1979 and nearly 75 percent of all households have had a close encounter with layoffs since 1980. Over 19 million people acknowledged that a lost job in their household had precipitated a major crisis in their lives. And when people we know lose their jobs, we often can't help but think, *"Could I be next?"* If *losing* a job, *keeping* a job, or *finding* another job are concerns, then this is the book for you.

In the last few years we have traveled throughout the world to speak to thousands of people at conferences, conventions, and company in-house workshops. Even though we both love to talk, we also love to listen. And we kept getting the same message from employees everywhere. They have told us they no longer knew what was expected of them. People who seemed to be doing their jobs well were being laid off, and no one understood the "new rules":

> Just what exactly is my company (or school, hospital, organization, association, etc.) looking for? What do they want me to do? I'm frustrated because there aren't enough clearly defined standards of what's expected of me. I don't understand how they decide which employees will keep their jobs and which ones won't.

Many employers and managers shared their employees' concerns:

> There are so many things we would like to say to our people, but we don't really know how to put it all into words. We haven't identified all the standards we should, and we're depending on vague descriptions in the employee handbook to do the work for us. And we admit, some of us are not skilled at clearly communicating what's important to us.

When we realized that many employers were not talking about what was expected of their employees, and that most employees had no guidelines for their future employability, we decided to do some research to try to bridge that gap. We interviewed hundreds of business owners, CEOs, managers, human resource directors, and supervisors, and posed this question to each of them:

> You have two employees, both technically competent, but you have to eliminate one of them due to downsizing, mergers, or budget constraints. What abilities or behaviors are you looking for to determine which employee will stay and which one will go?

In order to encourage these people to share their experiences, ideas, and opinions openly and honestly, we assured them that we would not identify them by name or company. Thus, you will notice that we do not cite specific organizations or companies, and use only the first names of the people we interviewed, sometimes even changing many of those to give them the anonymity they requested.

What we discovered in our survey is that CEOs, human resource executives, top-level managers, and supervisors are in remarkable agreement about the high-performance abilities they look for in determining which employees to hire, lay off, fire, or retain. There are eight of them. The key to staying successfully employed will depend upon your ability to:

1. Take Charge of Your Personal Life
2. Demonstrate Value Added
3. Have a Positive Impact on Your Company, Customers, and Colleagues
4. Embrace and Initiate Change
5. Work Harder, Smarter, Faster, and Better
6. Communicate Openly and Directly
7. Look for Leadership Opportunities
8. Commit to Lifelong Learning

Having or developing these eight abilities could very well save your career and allow you to stay employed. Notice we said "stay employed." We didn't say "keep the job you have now." There is a difference. Ironically, if your primary goal is to keep the job you have now, you may actually be placing yourself in jeopardy. We've observed that many employees who attempt to keep their current jobs often become anxious and resistant to change. They act defensively, hoard information that needs to be shared, and fear that they will lose credit for the work they do as part of a team. In other words, they display exactly the opposite behavior of what today's companies are looking for in a successful employee.

To stay employed, you have to picture yourself as "employable." With that aim in mind, our goal is to help you develop and use the high-performance abilities you need to be marketable and earn an income in an ever-changing world. As a first step, we urge you to be flexible and keep all your options open. These options could include being employed by another company or in another industry, working for more than one employer, moving to another department or location within your present company, or starting your own business. Keeping the job you have now is often only a short-term goal. Staying employed is a far-reaching, long-term goal.

John, one of the employees we interviewed, shared a personal example of the need to be flexible and adaptable in today's workplace:

> I had been employed with the same company for twenty-five years. When I turned fifty, I saw that full-time employment was no longer an option with my company. They were consolidating jobs, departments, titles, and people. So I used my knowledge and experience to outsource my skills to other companies. Now I work for one company three days a week, and another company two days a week. This is not how I had envisioned my job twenty-five years ago, but I've discovered I like the challenge, excitement, and change of pace that comes from working for two companies instead of one.

The future will see only a small percentage of people working until retirement for the same company. In fact, the U.S. Bureau of Labor Statistics predicts that every American worker will change careers—not jobs, but careers—at least three times throughout the course of his or her professional life. That means that most of us can no longer count on the safety net of a lifelong job. Many of the employees we interviewed wondered if there is *any* security left in the workplace these days. The answer is: *no*. And if job security as we have known it no longer exists, then it's up to each of us to create our own "career" security.

The supervisor of a retail department store told us, "Job security is no longer based on what the company gives you. It's based on what you give the company." And he defined "what you give the company" as making a visible contribution: becoming the person other employees want to have on their project team, having the confidence and self-assurance that comes with knowing your job and doing it well, and realizing you can do that job some-where else if the situation arises. But how do we go about making a visible contribution? The manager of a chemical refinery shared his opinion:

If you're my employee, it doesn't matter how long you've been on the job, how impressive your résumé is, or how many initials and titles come after your name. What matters is what you know, and how you continue to learn to stay on the cutting edge. How you apply that knowledge on the job is what really counts in our organization.

The CEO of a Fortune 500 company put it this way:

No one is going to take care of you today but yourself. Every employee focused on job security must be flexible and con-tribute to the bottom line—every single day.

Our research confirmed this reality. The only organization that will take people under its wing and guarantee them security for life is a state or federal penitentiary. Each of us must take respon-sibility for our lives—both personally and professionally. And we must plan for the future. There is no one else to blame if we fail to reach our goals. A mid-level manager commented:

We need people who are proactive and who look to the fu-ture—both their own future and the future of our organiza-tion. Our employees must be able to partner with us to stay one step ahead of the game, remain competitive in the chang-ing marketplace, break away from tired old ways of doing things, and help us plan for success.

Apart from the eight abilities that will make you employable, we must emphasize that every manager, CEO, human resource di-rector, supervisor, and business owner, without exception, stressed the importance of character. They all agreed that they wanted em-ployees they could trust, people who are compassionate and who incorporate in their lives and their jobs the values of honesty and integrity, people who keep their promises and who do what they say they are going to do.

Character might easily have become a separate chapter in this book. But the fact is that character permeates everything we do, everything we say, and everything we are. The other high-performance abilities we discuss are formed from a solid base of core values and strong character. They are the foundation upon which personal and professional success are built. So rather than a separate chapter on character in this book, you will find that high values, standards of excellence, and character are woven into every page of every chapter.

There is yet another factor in the workplace that may have an impact on the course of your career, one that both employees and employers were well aware of, but were reluctant to talk about: company politics. Based on what we heard, our advice to you in this area is to become savvy about the politics of your company, know the lay of the land, network accordingly, and understand that sometimes decisions are made which are not fair. This is another important reason to concentrate on long-term employability, rather than on simply keeping the job you have now.

We wish we could say that every company executive is completely fair, objective, and equitable in deciding who stays and who goes. But it is naive to think that if you close your eyes, cross your fingers, and keep your nose to the grindstone, all will be well. Sometimes, it is not enough to be good at your job. You must also stay connected and be alert, as illustrated by these two examples.

Dennis, a top-level manager in the utilities industry, knows about politics firsthand. His company had recently undergone a merger and he found himself being "reevaluated" and ranked among others from both the merging companies who were competing for his job. His results had been outstanding. Without a doubt, he was regarded as one of the top candidates. His division's financial results had risen impressively each year, and he felt confident that his record would count for something when the decision was made. An innovative and creative leader, he had developed a strong team using superb shared leadership techniques.

But Dennis had failed to take into account one important factor: politics. Another candidate got the job, even though he did not come close to matching Dennis's credentials or experience. However, he did have one important asset: he happened to be employed by the acquiring company which was now in charge.

What did Dennis do when he got the news? He complained about how unfair it was, retreated for a while, felt sorry for himself, and worried about his future and the future of his family—all in a matter of a few days. Then, being the professional he was, he picked himself up and took a long, hard look at his options. He had been wise enough to develop a strong network of friends and colleagues, and he began contacting them. Word spread, as it always does when someone good is available, and soon the phone began to ring. Dennis's comfortable existence may have changed, but his reputation, integrity, and character had not. He now has an excellent job and says with a smile, "This is a whole new ball game, and I just hit a home run!"

Contrast that success story with Jill's experience when her company went through a major downsizing effort:

> I never dreamed my company would let me go in a million years. Many of my co-workers took advantage of the voluntary buyout offer, but I decided to hang in there because I thought I knew the right people and I just knew they would keep me! Then I had to meet with a special committee and prove to them that I brought value to the company and was an integral part of helping it make a profit. When I couldn't do that to their satisfaction, I was told they would no longer be needing my services.

Did Jill react as optimistically and professionally as Dennis? Unfortunately, she didn't. When we asked what her options were, she replied grimly:

> Not so good. My current severance package is not nearly as valuable as the voluntary buyout. I do have unlimited access to the resource center, which is supposed to provide me with

job counseling, use of office space and equipment, and access to a database of job postings at other companies. I went a few times, but it's too depressing. It's just a roomful of perky, upbeat career counselors (who all have jobs) and a lot of depressed employees who are still in shock. When I think of all the networking doors I closed behind me over the years, because I was so sure my job was secure, I could kick myself.

No matter how good you are, your job may be history for a variety of reasons that make no sense to you. We can't promise that reading this book will guarantee you will keep your present job, but it could very well guarantee your future employability. Perhaps the most important question is: "What will you do with the information and strategies we will share with you?" It's amazing how many people will read a book from cover to cover, dutifully highlight the important parts, take notes, and then do nothing. Why? Because changing is hard work! So many people want easy answers. Unfortunately, there are no easy answers if you want to stay employed.

Many employees we talked to were so busy trying to find fault or blame someone for their recent or impending job loss that they couldn't focus on doing something about remaining employable. Their anger, frustration, and bitterness drained them of the excitement, creativity, and energy they needed to move in a positive direction. This book is not about fault or blame. It's about the eight high-performance abilities you need to stay employed. We could argue at length about whether a company has the right to expect these abilities from their employees. But arguing will not change the reality of today's workplace. These abilities are, in fact, what today's companies expect of employees.

We're not saying that you *have* to meet these expectations. But we do recommend that you seriously consider the importance of these abilities if you want to stay employed. Your job title and job duties may change, you may leave your present company through downsizing or through your own choice. You may already have some or even all of these abilities. But if you do not, are you willing to change your behavior to fit the needs of today's employers?

It's been said that the main reason people are willing to undergo serious change is because they realize it's imperative to their survival to do so. In today's volatile and rapidly changing workplace, it is indeed imperative to our survival that we become—and remain—as marketable as possible. Without a doubt, we can no longer depend on a company or an organization for our financial and professional well-being. Instead, we must learn to depend on ourselves. Each of us must be responsible for our own professional future. So get ready to explore in detail the answer to the most frequently asked question in these increasingly uncertain times:

▣ "What abilities or behaviors must I have or develop in order to stay employed?"

CHAPTER 1

Take Charge of Your Personal Life

▣ Which employee would I keep? I want people working for me who come to work ready to get the job done—people whose personal life is stable enough that they can direct their attention and energy to their work, their customers, and their teammates.

It may come as a surprise that all the CEOs, human resource directors, managers, and business owners we interviewed agreed that the quality and stability of an employee's personal life often have a direct impact upon the quality and success of his or her professional life. Why? Because in many ways, your professional life mirrors your personal life. For example, if you are continually late for work, you are probably late for your personal appointments as well. If you dislike having to work as part of a team, then you probably also have difficulty with carpools, club committees, and church groups. If you usually resist and resent taking orders or directions from a manager or employer, chances are you have always had trouble with the authority figures in your life. You are who you are twenty-four hours a day—at home or at work.

Often employees will say to us: "I don't understand what my

personal life has to do with work. It's called personal because it's private and it's nobody else's business!" True, we couldn't agree more. Your personal life *is* private—if you leave it at home. However, according to the CEOs and managers we interviewed, many employees do not keep their personal lives private. Instead, they bring their personal problems into the workplace, thus affecting their ability to do their job well. Roger, a director of pharmacy for a large drugstore chain, told us:

> I feel like I'm involved in a soap opera at work. Every single day, one employee or another seems to be going through a major life crisis that not only affects their work, but everyone else's. To be a successful manager nowadays, you almost have to be a counselor, pastor, therapist, parent, and financial advisor. I spend more time consoling, cajoling, sympathizing, and listening to my employees' problems than I do planning more effective ways to run my store. I have problems, too, but I don't bring them to work and dump them on my employees.

Most managers we spoke to made similar comments about how much time they spend counseling employees about their personal lives. Not only were they losing valuable work time, but they felt inadequate to provide the type of help their employees needed. We always discourage managers from becoming their employees' counselor, therapist, parent, or pastor. First, they do not have the knowledge or experience to take on those roles. And second, it is not their job. We encourage them instead to suggest to their employees that they look for appropriate resources within their own community to get whatever help they may need. It is important to recognize that managers are uncomfortable with, and sometimes even resentful of, the demands made upon them to become overly involved in some of their employees' personal lives.

A participant in a recent workshop commented: "I still don't understand. What's the big deal? If I come to work and do my job, it's nobody's business if I have a terrible home life or if my spouse drinks too much." Again, we agree; it is nobody else's business—as long as such circumstances in no way affect this employee's ability to do her job effectively. But, unfortunately, that is often not the case.

When I (Connie) was Director of Employee Assistance and Staff Relations for a major hospital, I was often asked to counsel employees whose performance at work did not meet the hospital's expectations. These problems came in many forms: insubordination, resisting change, being rude to a patient or family members, complaining, gossiping, tattling—the list was endless. As I investigated further, I discovered that an employee's behavior at work could usually be traced to a problem in his or her personal life such as an impending divorce, a family member who was using drugs, a physically abusive spouse, an uncommunicative adolescent, a child who was doing poorly in school, or aging parents who could no longer take care of themselves. Unquestionably, the quality of a person's life outside of work has a great impact on the quality of his or her life at work. Listen to what a public utilities employee told us:

I've always been a private person. I can take care of myself. I've been going through a very difficult divorce, but felt confident that I was handling everything fine and leaving these problems at home. But my manager told me last week that customers have been complaining about me. They've said I've been impatient, even rude at times. I have to admit that the fact their electricity is out for a few hours does not seem very important compared to what I am going through trying to fight for custody of my five-year-old daughter. I guess my customers are picking up on those feelings. When I told my manager what was going on, he was very understanding, but he was still committed to the customer getting the best service possible. We've worked out a temporary schedule where, for the next couple of months, I'll have less telephone contact and work on a couple of computer projects instead. I realize now that my personal life does affect my work, even when I am trying my best to hide it.

Two areas of our personal life have a major impact upon our professional life: our current relationships and our childhood experiences. In our conversations with employees, we have found that the people who felt safe, supported, and loved at home and within their personal relationships could weather many storms at work. With the support of family and friends, most people can overcome difficult obstacles at work, including transferring to a new department, leaving a job they love, going back to school to learn new procedures, or simply standing up to the office bully. An employee, who recently lost his job as a result of downsizing, said:

> I could not have made it through this without my family and friends. First of all, they understood how much this job really meant to me. I definitely needed some sympathy from friends who would allow me to wallow a bit in a little self-pity about how unfair this was. But as all good friends and family do, they didn't let me stay down for long. They quickly worked to get me to put this behind me and move on. They sent cartoons, left jokes on my answering machine, and kept me busy. They have all helped me realize that I didn't lose what is really important—the people I love.

Because employees must often deal with difficult or imperfect people, as well as with a changing work environment and new technology, it's going to be almost impossible to be effective on the job if they have major personal problems that are unresolved. The future will require more focus on work, more flexibility, more willingness to work as a team, more risk-taking, and more energy. Employees must feel good about themselves and come to work excited and ready, rather than emotionally drained from hours of conflict, sadness, or abuse at home. It has been our experience that people who cannot find the courage, strength, willpower, or assertiveness to work on resolving personal problems also have a difficult time coping with the overwhelming changes and demands of the workplace today.

Jennifer, a young assistant manager in a retail store, talked about one of her employees who was struggling with an abusive marriage:

> We can tell the moment she walks into the store what kind of night she had, because she's rude to customers and short-tempered with her co-workers. I know it's hard to be in an abusive relationship and still be a top salesperson. I sympathize with her situation, but she has refused all offers of help and counseling. I've done my best for her, but I also have a store to run. The accountants who tally my sales figures at the end of each month don't take my employees' personal lives into consideration. My upcoming promotion depends on my ability to generate higher sales at this store. I'm a single parent with a small child to support. I cannot afford to let my employee's inability to do her job affect my chance to move ahead.

Unfortunately, this employee's personal life has not only affected her ability to do her job, but it has also had a negative impact on her supervisor, her co-workers, and her customers. Few companies can afford to allow a situation like this to continue for too long.

Most of us spend a lifetime reacting in one way or another to childhood experiences, and we often imitate the attitudes and behaviors of the adults and caregivers of our youth. Brian, the foreman in a rural industrial plant, has already seen an example of this in one of his employees:

> John, one of my supervisors, would scream at everyone—including secretaries, workers, vendors, and customers—whenever something went wrong. Then my boss explained to me that when John's dad was a supervisor at this plant years ago, he behaved in exactly the same way. Okay. So now I understand why John acts this way. He learned it from watching his dad. But that doesn't make it right. He's got to stop it. He's got to learn to change his approach. We've already lost

a hardworking secretary and a valued customer because of John's tirades. I discussed this with John and I told him directly that he is not his father and that he must choose to react differently because his job is in jeopardy.

Think about the people who surrounded you as a child: your parents and grandparents, family members, teachers, religious leaders, and other adults. These are the people who contributed to your becoming the person you are today. If you respected them as role models and learned from them, you probably have tried to emulate the values they taught you and carry on the traditions they instilled in you. But if you did not respect the people who raised you, you probably have no desire to be like them and you have had to work hard to break old patterns and create a new life for yourself and your family based on the values and traditions that you do admire and respect. That is often difficult because the feelings associated with past experiences can come to the surface without warning. And unfortunately, there is always the tendency to assimilate some of the attitudes and prejudices of the people who raised us.

Yet, regardless of the past, each of us can choose the kind of life we want to build for ourselves and our families. We can allow past experiences, negative feelings, prejudices, put-downs, and myths to affect our present-day behavior, or we can decide to reprogram ourselves with new, more positive directives. If changes are necessary and we are willing to make them, then we have taken the first step toward taking charge of our lives.

Without a doubt, our present personal experiences and relationships are just as important as our childhood ones. How is your current personal life situation? Are you in a relationship where you feel safe? Do family members and close friends support you? Are your relationships addiction free? Are you encouraged to do your best, and do others let you know they are proud of you? How do you feel about yourself?

It is important to remember that we will be treated exactly as we believe we deserve to be treated. Why? Because people will read the signals we send out and get the message about our level of confidence, how we feel about ourselves, and our sense of self-worth and self-esteem. It's as though we all have a big sign around our necks that describes exactly how we will allow ourselves to be treated. Here are examples of some "signs" you might read from people you know, at home or on the job:

- ▣ "I'm a good, loving person. I'll be a good friend. But I do have limits and expect to be treated respectfully."

- ▣ "I don't want to fight, argue, or have any kind of confrontation. If you don't like something, it's probably my fault. I'm sorry."

Do either of these sound familiar? As you begin to read the signs others are wearing, what do you see? And what does your sign say about how you feel about yourself and how you expect to be treated?

Self-esteem is one of the most important signals we can send. It is the radiating force that allows us to experience events, people, and situations as participators rather than as victims. Self-esteem is the key to a life full of choices. Confident people believe that through their words and actions they can choose how they will respond to the people and events in their lives.

Several employees we interviewed had definite ideas on the subject of choice. Robert said: "Choices? Oh, sure. Should I choose 'Life A' or 'Life B'? 'Life A' gives me a future in which my wife leaves me, my child uses drugs, and I lose my job. 'Life B' gives me everything I could ever hope for, so I think I'll choose 'Life B.' Let's get real! It doesn't work that way!"

It's true. If it were simply a matter of deciding on the quality of our relationships and the direction in which we wanted our lives to go, none of us would purposely choose to have a life full of problems. But making the choice to assess our beliefs, attitudes, perceptions, and behaviors is the necessary first step toward successful change. The second and most difficult step is taking the actions necessary to make that choice a reality. This often requires a great deal of hard work, training, education, and sometimes even counseling.

I (Connie) will always remember a young woman I counseled for several months. Dorothy wasn't happy in her job or her marriage. She had dropped out of high school in her senior year, and had a low-paying job. When I began to talk to Dorothy about evaluating herself and the changes she would like to make in her life, she quickly responded, "This isn't about me. It's about my ex-husband, my kids, my customers, my co-workers, and how unfair everything is." There was the problem, that time-honored excuse: "It's not me. It's everybody else."

"Dorothy," I explained, "I can't help them, but I can help you take charge of your life. That will require us to focus on you. Do you want to take control of your life?"

"Oh, yes," she replied tearfully, "but I don't even know where to begin. It all seems so overwhelming."

Change can be overwhelming, but it's not impossible. Through counseling, Dorothy began to understand, perhaps for the first time in her life, the importance of assuming responsibility for herself. When I asked her what she wanted most, she answered without hesitation, "I want to leave my job. But I can't afford to. I'm a single mom."

My answer to her was, "If that is what you want, then let's focus on that as your goal. Now, what steps do you have to take so you can leave your job and find something else you want to do?" We developed a plan so she could earn her high school equivalency diploma and start college with financial assistance. That would enable her to develop the skills she needed to leave her present job and become employable in another business.

Dorothy put her plan into action and as she began to take charge of her life, our appointments became further and further apart until she stopped coming altogether. A year later, I saw her at a conference. She looked great—happy, physically fit, and very professional. When I asked if she had quit her job, which had been her original goal, she said, "Oh, no! I love my job!"

"That isn't how you felt a year ago," I said. "What happened?"

"Well," she replied, "I finished school and learned the new

skills I needed to keep current. I got a promotion and I'm getting along well with my co-workers. I have friends at work, I serve on a couple of volunteer committees, and I really enjoy what I'm doing. Quit my job? Absolutely not!"

This is your life, your one opportunity to be the best you can be and accomplish what it is you choose to do. You have the right to be safe, free, productive, respected, loved, and happy. But creating this kind of life for yourself takes hard work. We are continually amazed at the number of people who believe they are entitled to be happy every moment of every day. And some of them also believe they are entitled to a paycheck simply because they show up for work. No one is entitled to anything. What about you? Are you content and happy with your personal relationships? Your work relationships? Your job? Your life? If not, what are you doing to change that? How do you feel you deserve to be treated? Do you convey your feelings to others? Are you determined to work hard and pursue your goals or do you just complain about how unlucky you are? Have you accepted and acted upon the belief that you have choices about how to live your life? These questions are important ones if you are to develop and maintain a positive personal life.

Making a choice is not always easy, especially when it involves making major changes. Often a choice means harder work ahead, and sometimes making a decision is difficult because none of the choices available are desirable. I (Jean) faced this kind of situation when my sister Patty was diagnosed with a very rare—and sometimes fatal—kidney disease at the age of twenty-seven. After carefully considering all her options, she finally decided to undergo a transplant. This option was a very frightening and risky one, because twenty years ago transplants were not the everyday procedure they are today. And Patty's choice involved another person: me.

When Patty asked me to donate one of my kidneys, I had a tough decision to make. Actually I only had two choices: yes or no. Even though Patty was my sister, I had to consider my husband and our two small children. I also had a very responsible position at work, and I didn't know how my employer and my co-workers would react to my extended leave of absence for the surgery and recovery time. Based on all the information we both had, Patty and I made the right decision for us. I donated a kidney; the transplant was a great success, and everything worked out well. My employer, colleagues, family, and friends couldn't have been more supportive.

We all have to make our share of tough calls. But many people have told us they live their lives in constant indecision, never making a move in either direction, yet struggling where they are. When we asked why they put off making decisions, here are the reasons they gave:

1. They can't decide what's the best thing to do;
2. They know what's best, but they can't face the hard work and/or difficult consequences their decision may bring;
3. They hope that by waiting (and procrastinating) the decision may get easier;
4. They hope someone else will make the decision for them; or
5. If they wait long enough, the decision will take care of itself and they won't have to do anything after all.

We encourage people like that to see that moving toward *some* goal is usually preferable to making no decision at all and remaining stuck in the same place. What about you? Take a look at what's happening in your personal life and in your personal relationships. Examine what's going on in your professional life. Are you putting off making an important decision that could affect your personal and/or professional life? If you are, we have only two questions for you:

1. What's keeping you from making the decision you know must be made?
2. Won't putting off an important decision eventually make it even harder to decide?

What about the employee who asks, "But aren't there times in our lives when circumstances beyond our control may affect our ability to do our best on the job?" Of course. Life brings uncertainties and stressful situations that can touch us and affect us so strongly that our jobs and the expectations that come with them seem almost irrelevant. In our research we discovered that most companies not only understand, but are willing to make arrangements to help employees through these difficult times. One CEO explained his philosophy:

> The more employees we add, the more personal problems we expect. That's just logical, based on percentages ... but we will do everything we can to help an employee who is going through a rough time.

Although many of the CEOs and managers we interviewed showed compassion and a willingness to help employees, they also had certain expectations.

1. They expect employees to try to deal with their personal problems on their own and to ask for help only with the most serious problems;

2. They expect employees to make every reasonable effort to get help if they need it;

3. They expect employees to work with them to find a solution such as a temporary replacement or a new work schedule, so they can continue to provide the best service to their customers while they work together with their employees to deal with their problems.

Let's look at these three expectations more closely and examine how you can meet them.

1. SEPARATE THE "BIG" STUFF FROM THE "LITTLE" STUFF

If an employee is constantly upset, depressed, stressed, or involved in a life "emergency," the employer's patience will finally wear thin. The manager of a large travel agency told us about one such employee:

> To hear her talk, you would think she's the only one who has ever had trouble in her marriage or problems with her kids. At first we tried to help by listening, covering for her so she could have time off, and excusing her when she snapped at co-workers or customers. But it's been a year and there's no end in sight. We've also realized that most of her so-called problems are not that big. Many of us are dealing with problems similar to hers, but we don't let it affect our work. We simply cannot continue to keep her on the payroll. We can handle one crisis every now and then, but we can't allow her to continue with this "crisis of the week" attitude.

Companies cannot and should not be expected to accept a drop in work performance for every stressful event that comes along. Employers must be able to count on their employees to deal with most situations on their own, most of the time, without affecting their ability to have a positive impact on their customers and co-workers. What about you? Can you separate the "little" stuff from the "big" stuff? If you can, then you have a right to expect that your company will respond with compassion and provide the assistance you need when a major crisis occurs.

2. GET HELP IF YOU NEED IT

Raising and educating our children in a drug-free environment, providing for aging parents, losing some or all of our possessions in a natural disaster, facing financial problems, dealing with the death of a loved one, and facing a life-threatening illness are just a few of the issues with which all of us may struggle at some point in our lives. But as understanding as employers may be, they can only do so much in such situations. It is the employees' responsibility to themselves and to their company to make every effort possible to work through the trauma and emotional impact caused by the serious events in their lives, even if it means getting help from outside sources.

Sometimes people think that asking for support and help is a sign of weakness, that they should be "strong" enough to work through grief, pain, fear, and/or depression on their own. We have found the opposite to be true. Weak people rarely ask for help. For the most part, people who do seek help tend to be very strong and very determined not to become victims of abuse, neglect, violence, or tragedy. They may have been momentarily "weakened" by a specific event, but it was their strength of purpose and character that led them to seek the help and support that would allow them to heal and move on.

The hardest thing for many of us to do is to admit we need help. What about you? Are you a person who can ask for help when you need it? Are you unwilling to be a victim of circumstance and actively search for ways to cope with even the "big" things that come your way? If your personal life is in trouble or out of control, then perhaps you could benefit from some of the many excellent services available in your community or through your own company. Whether you solve your problem yourself or with the help of others, the results are worth the effort: peace of mind, healthier relationships, a new outlook on life, and, of course, better on-the-job performance.

3. WORK WITH YOUR COMPANY TO FIND A SOLUTION

When employees realize their personal circumstances are hindering their ability to do their jobs effectively, they have an obligation to let their manager or employer know as soon as possible. Trying to keep it a secret or hoping no one will notice might increase the stress already induced by the event. Companies will be more compassionate and willing to help if they are made aware of the situation before the problem begins to affect customers or the productivity of the other people on the team and in the workplace. The manager of a recycling plant told us about an employee who handled a crisis very professionally:

Mary came into my office and by the look on her face, I knew immediately that something was wrong, because she takes everything in stride and rarely gets upset. She had just found out her husband had cancer. Before I could even begin to tell her how sorry I was, she began to explain "her plan." While her husband was hospitalized for the two weeks following his surgery, Mary wanted to leave work an hour early each day to be with him. She had already talked to another employee who agreed to work that extra hour. In exchange, Mary would come in early each day to pick up an hour of the other employee's shift. She handed me a schedule as well as important information for her replacement. I was so impressed! Even in a crisis, she had taken the responsibility to make sure her job was covered. We were anxious to help Mary, and we worked with her throughout the next few weeks. When employees care that much about us, there isn't anything we wouldn't do for them in return.

Even though your company may sympathize with your plight, it is not the company's responsibility to solve the problem. It is your responsibility to work with your company to find a way to deal with the problem in the best way for both you and your employer.

Of course, no one's personal life is ever perfectly in order, because we all live in an imperfect world. As quickly as we resolve one problem, another one may be right around the corner. That's precisely why we must have good, loving, solid relationships in other areas of our lives to help us through problem times. What about you? What needs to happen in your personal relationships to give you a calm center from which to function effectively on the job? Can you separate the "big" stuff from the "little" stuff? Are you confident enough even to admit you have problems? Are you strong enough to ask for help if you cannot resolve them yourself?

Today's organizations expect employees to come to work ready to put their full effort and energy into the task at hand. Never underestimate the countless ways in which your personal life has an impact on your professional life. Maintaining good personal relationships, taking an active approach to decision-making, and working hard to make your choices a reality are all important keys to your success in the workplace. You have the power to make your personal life one you can be proud of. And your well-ordered personal life will be reflected in your work and in your ability to ensure your future employability.

CHAPTER 2

Demonstrate Value Added

▣ Which employees would I keep? The ones who realize that every decision, idea, action, and plan must be linked to the long-term financial stability and growth of our company. I need to keep employees who are determined to add unique personal value in pursuit of that goal.

What we heard in our interviews with CEOs, managers, and human resource directors was their firm belief that employability is based first and foremost on each employee's answer to this most important question:

▣ What added value do you bring to your job that directly contributes to the financial stability, success, and growth of our company?

Your future will depend on your ability to answer this question. Can you demonstrate to those people who make the hiring and firing decisions that you do bring added value to your company? A business owner shared this observation:

We are looking for employees who not only understand the need for us to remain profitable but who are actively involved in finding ways to increase profits. This is certainly the kind of employee we want to keep on board, and it's definitely the kind of employee we need.

A human resource director told us:

There was a time in our company when we would keep people on staff because of extenuating circumstances. They were decent folks who needed their jobs. We wanted to keep them, and we could afford to carry them along. But times have changed, and we don't have that luxury anymore. Every person must contribute to the bottom line. As head of human resources, I am now in a position where I must convince the board that every job on the payroll is absolutely necessary for our company to continue to grow.

In many of today's big companies, the problem is that the decision-makers are often not aware of the contributions of individual employees. So it is up to each employee to document and demonstrate his or her own value. We have heard many stories about enthusiastic and intelligent men and women who communicated effectively, exhibited strong leadership skills, embraced change, and worked efficiently yet still found themselves among the ranks of the unemployed. It wasn't because they lacked the technical competence or the interpersonal skills needed to do the job. It was because they simply could not—or were not given the opportunity to—persuade those in power that their job was *vital* to the continued success and growth of their company.

The word "vital" means necessary to existence, essential. Taken in that context, vital could very well be one of the most important words in today's changing workplace. Could you convince your company that you and your job are essential components that are necessary—even essential—to help it reach its goals? If your manager invited you into his office tomorrow, closed the door, and asked you the question we posed earlier—"*What added value do you bring to your job that directly contributes to the financial stability, success, and growth of our company?"*—how would you respond? We assure you, this is *not* a hypothetical question. It's one that is being asked in real-life companies every single day. And it will be asked of you—if not now, then at some time in the future. To be totally prepared, you must think long and hard about your job and your place within your company and develop an answer that is strong and persuasive. There is no doubt that your ability to respond to this question can and will determine your future employability.

When we posed this question to employees, we found many of them had a difficult time responding for several reasons:

1. Many believe that "doing only what's required" is good enough. They have not yet realized that employability today is based on far more than simply doing one's job as it is spelled out in the "job description."

2. They don't see themselves and their jobs as being directly linked to the ongoing financial success of their company. They concentrate only on their own specific responsibilities and do not see themselves and their jobs in relation to the big picture.

3. They don't understand the importance of documenting their performance and keeping track of the "extras" that extend beyond their specific jobs.

4. Uncomfortable with "blowing their own horn," they do not share their ideas, strategies, and successes. Although their jobs may be necessary, they are reluctant to convince the decision-makers in their company of that fact.

All of these beliefs and attitudes are self-limiting and self-defeating. Many CEOs, human resource directors, managers, and business owners told us about employees who did their jobs adequately but fell short when it came to *visibly* demonstrating their value to the company. To remain employable, your number one goal must be to prove to your company (or a potential employer, if you are seeking employment) that you *do* add value because you are (or will be) vital and essential to helping them reach their goals. And the simple fact is that beneath all the rhetoric, slogans, and mission statements the primary goal of every business is to make a profit. In not-for-profit organizations, "making a profit" means staying financially sound.

People often say to us, "But making a profit is not my main motivator. I feel what I do is important and I believe my job allows me the opportunity to provide a service or product that customers want and need." And we found that sentiment to be true of most of the employees we interviewed. When we address CEOs, business owners, and managers we stress that although their number one goal is to remain sound, they must understand this is not the primary goal of their employees or their customers. Surveys show that employees want, more than anything, to feel that their work is meaningful and appreciated. Customers want quality, value, and service. The successful companies with whom we work know how to make a profit while effectively meeting the needs of their employees and their customers.

On the other hand, employees must never forget for a moment that their company's number one goal is to make a profit. No matter what your business or industry, you must be able to prove that you are a valuable asset to your company and demonstrate how you and your job are linked to their number one goal. If you can help your company make money and/or help your company save money, then your chances of staying employed are high.

HELP YOUR COMPANY MAKE MONEY

In our global and highly competitive marketplace, it's not as easy for companies to make a profit as it was in the past. A marketing vice president commented:

Technology has increased our access to information and produced very knowledgeable consumers. It has become difficult to corner a market because "tricks of the trade" are learned and copied quickly by our competitors, and "trade secrets" don't stay secret for very long. Industries are abandoning their niches and moving into new arenas. We have competition now from entities that did not compete with us until a few years ago.

Evidence from communities nationwide proves that these words are right on target. Gas stations sell groceries and grocery stores sell drugs and cosmetics. Drugstores now sell lawn furniture and greeting cards, banks sell insurance, and clothing stores sell jewelry. These are just a few examples of how customers can buy the same product or service from a wide variety of providers at very competitive prices. How, then, does one company or organization prevail above the rest in order to make the profits necessary for its growth and even its very survival? Scott, a training and education director for a large company, explained it this way:

> How does a buyer decide which provider to use if the quality and price are comparable? The determining factor in that decision will be the extra value added by one seller that the customer wants and the others do not offer.

If a company is committed to making money by providing top-quality products and services along with extra value to its customers, then to be successful employees must demonstrate how their jobs contribute to that pursuit. They can do that by retaining the customers they already have and/or bringing in new customers.

The value you bring to your company will almost always be directly related to the positive impact you have on your company's customers. If you do not have some direct customer contact, or work with those who do, there is a high probability that your job will not be perceived as vital in the near future. The customer ultimately determines the success of every organization and its ability to make a profit. Sam Walton, founder of Wal-Mart, commented: "There is only one boss—the customer. And he can fire everybody in the company from the chairman on down, simply by spending his money somewhere else."

Amazingly, many companies forget that the customer is the absolute determining factor in their profitability—or lack of it. In their rush to increase profits quickly, they fail to include customer value and satisfaction in their formula for success. Companies on the cutting edge understand the crucial difference between short-term and long-term profits. The former CEO of a failed financial institution told us:

> Stockholders were unhappy with our bottom line, so we tried to increase profits by launching an extensive downsizing campaign. Things looked good for a while, but then we found ourselves having to cut more jobs a few months later. We learned too late that fewer employees meant we could not continue to provide the quality of service our customers had come to expect. So they left us for our competition. A vicious cycle developed: profits dropped, more layoffs followed, service suffered, and more customers left. Now all of us are unemployed.

Another ex-CEO told us that his company had tried to increase its cash flow by decreasing the quality of its product. His company soon went out of business. Successful companies that show solid and consistent long-term profits, sustained growth, and high productivity are those whose bottom-line goal is far more visionary than simply making a quick profit. These companies have a strategic plan that motivates them to produce sustained long-term profits without compromising quality, staff, or service. This goal can be accomplished only by a total company-wide commitment to customer service. Cutting staff and reducing quality may solve the immediate cash flow problems or show a drastic increase in profits. But long-term profitability is now, and always will be, directly related to a company's ability to maintain a loyal customer base.

This means that every employee—including the mail room clerks, receptionists, clerical staff, accountants, service representatives, maintenance personnel, and everyone else who collects a paycheck—must be 100 percent committed to bringing in new customers and keeping the ones they have. Peter, the manager of a large sporting goods store, told us about an employee who did this exceptionally well.

> LeAnne earns her salary twice over. She is always coming up with ideas we can use to promote or market a new piece of equipment. Last month she helped design a promotion piece in our city newspaper that literally packed our store with buying customers. We sold out of the product in three hours.

LeAnne was not even a full-time employee. She was a college student who came in on weekends to help put flyers on the windshields of cars in the parking lot. While she was passing out the flyers, she came up with the idea for the promotion piece. She is a good example of how an employee, no matter what his or her official job title, can contribute to a company's success by helping to bring in new customers.

While it's important to bring in new customers, loyal customers will always generate the greatest source of revenue. Acquiring new customers is not only time-consuming, but it also costs money and lowers profits. New customers are only valuable in the long run if a company can keep them coming back. The sales manager for a medical equipment company told us:

> We used to offer sales commissions based on new customer acquisitions. But we soon realized that our sales force was always working to obtain new business, instead of concentrating on servicing the customers we already had. Soon, some of our more loyal customers went with another company who provided outstanding service. Now we focus on taking care of our VIPs, those valued customers who have stayed with us over time. Through word-of-mouth marketing to their associates, they bring us all the new customers we need.

Many employees think their jobs have nothing to do with serving customers. Deanna, a systems analyst, commented:

Customers? I never even see a customer! All I do is work at a computer terminal all day. I input data we receive from our customer surveys, analyze the results, and send the reports out to all our store managers. How can I prove my job is needed when I never even leave my office and this computer?

Deanna is failing to see how she fits into the big picture. Of course her job has an impact on customers! Her analysis and input can change the direction of her company's marketing plan, the focus of its service strategy, and even the nature of the product or service it provides. And there are similar examples in every business. An assembly line worker helps to produce a quality product that customers will enjoy using again and again. A chef can make or break a restaurant's reputation by the quality of the food he prepares and his ability to cooperate with the other kitchen staff, as well as the waiters who do interact directly with customers. Even if you don't have direct customer contact, you must be able to demonstrate your ability to work directly and cooperatively with those employees who do.

A purchasing agent for a large retail chain agreed:

Mark, a member of my department, does not have direct customer contact, but he works with employees who do. He doesn't seem to realize that his lack of organization and time-liness affect their ability to service our customers well. He fails to see how his job is one piece of a much larger picture. We need employees with more foresight about servicing customers, even if they are not directly in contact with them.

Arlene, an investment specialist who works directly with customers, shared a frustrating example of a lack of support from someone on her team:

Each investment officer was given a computer-generated list of new contacts we were supposed to make. I was excited and came to work ready to identify new leads and make some sales. But I soon discovered that my list had outdated addresses and phone numbers, and nothing about the potential client's occupation. I spent most of my day looking up basic information that should have been provided on the list to begin with. I wasn't able to call on one new client that day. When I complained to my co-worker about the poor quality of the list she had generated, her comment was, "Well, I didn't want to do the list anyway. After all, it's your job to contact customers—not mine."

This "behind the scenes" employee failed to realize that she did indeed have a customer—the investment officer for whom she generated that outdated report. Do you have direct customer contact? If not, are you working with people who do? What impact does *your* job have on their ability to do *their* job? And whether or not you have direct customer contact, to stay employable your job must bring added value in the form of profits to your company.

Help your company save money

A company can also increase profits by saving money, which is the reason for all the downsizing, cutbacks, and layoffs that are occurring in industries and businesses nationwide. What every employee must understand is that there are only five ways for a company to save money.

1. Reduce staff
2. Cut benefits
3. Lower wages
4. Decrease quality of products or services
5. Increase productivity

Employees don't want their companies to eliminate jobs, slash benefits, or cut wages. And customers definitely do not want reduced levels of quality and service. Therefore, the only other way to save money (and make money at the same time) is to increase productivity. In other words, working harder and producing more are the only options that will allow an employee to continue working for the same compensation and benefits in today's marketplace. Yet many employees fail to understand this basic and very important concept. Edward, a department manager for an insurance company, said:

> Our company just went through a major downsizing. I managed to keep my job with the same salary and benefits, but they've assigned me extra responsibilities. Now three of us are doing the work that four of us did a month ago. I'm not going to put up with this! I told the others we shouldn't work any harder than before, and once the company discovers we can't do the job, they will just have to hire another person.

Obviously, Edward does not understand the big picture. The only way for his company to cut costs to save money and continue to make a profit was to increase the workload of the employees who were left after downsizing. This company is not prepared to hire another person. It is prepared, however, to replace Edward with someone who would be glad to have a job with his salary and benefits.

Employees often become frustrated by changes in their organizational structure. They are worried about their jobs and their future. They are tired of extra work with fewer people and resources. That is understandable, but they must be careful not to let these feelings affect their job performance. A married couple, Marilyn and Eric, are employed by different companies which are going through similar changes. Both spouses are facing the real possibility of being laid off. Marilyn commented:

> I come to work and do my job—no more, no less. But I am not going to do one extra thing. I simply do what's required. If they think they can put me through all this worry about my job and then expect me to work harder, they can just forget it.

Eric expressed similar feelings:

> I do what I have to do to get by. No extra projects and committees for me. If this company thinks it can treat us like this and then expect us to jump at the chance to "be more involved," they are badly mistaken.

Marilyn and Eric are expressing their anger, worries, and frustrations by cutting back on their productivity. They are operating under the myth that their companies owe them the guarantee of a job, and now were failing to keep their promise and their part of the bargain. What promise? What bargain? Marilyn and Eric answered emphatically and without hesitation:

> We both may lose our jobs! We've given our companies some of the best years of our lives, and look at what they've given us in return.

Interestingly enough, Marilyn and Eric act as though their employment has been a one-way street, as if they were the only ones who fulfilled their end of the bargain. Let's take a look at just what their companies did give them in return for their years on the job. They paid their mortgage, put their kids through school, and provided health care for their entire family. They both got paid for ten "sick days" when they did not come to work, and they each received fourteen days with full pay for their vacations. Their paychecks put food on their table, two cars in their garage, and furnished their home. Obviously, their companies did fulfill their end of the bargain, which is this: an employee goes to work, does a good job, and in return is paid a fair salary plus benefits. *Nowhere* was there any sort of promise or guarantee that more than that should be expected or provided.

We Americans are compassionate people, but perhaps we've gotten spoiled. Most companies have tried to do the best by their employees and have often made a sincere attempt to keep them on the payroll—no matter what. But like Marilyn and Eric, instead of appreciating their efforts and seeing this as a fair trade, many people have come to see employment as a right to which they are entitled.

Entitlement is out, and pay for performance is in. This is not the time to decrease your productivity. Most companies are asking more from their employees because they are trying to eliminate as few jobs as possible, keep wages and benefits stable, and also make a profit. Employees who decrease their productivity are ensuring that their company will have to make more cutbacks.

If you want to stay employed, this is not the time to let your confusion, bitterness, apathy, anger, or downright stubbornness cause you to reduce your productivity. Your efforts to work harder with less support and fewer resources will usually be noticed and appreciated. One CEO said:

In order for our division to survive with the increased competition for our product, we had to concentrate on ways to save money. We were committed to keeping our staff intact and we were also determined to keep our employees' wages and benefits the same. So we needed to produce more with the workforce we had. I am so very proud of our people! After we explained our situation, they all pitched in with cooperation and enthusiasm. As a result, we got through a bad period and our profit numbers look great. To thank the employees who made this turnaround possible, we divided a percentage of profits and were able to surprise our staff with generous bonus checks.

Besides increasing productivity, employees can help their company save money by creatively integrating money-saving ideas into their jobs. A restaurant manager told us this story:

Each week as I took inventory, I noticed we were always missing silverware. A fork here and a spoon there doesn't sound like much, but it adds up after a while and replacing those missing items costs money. One day, one of our busboys, Jonathan, told me he had noticed silverware was often accidentally tossed in the garbage when they emptied the trays with dirty dishes. He suggested that the servers separate the silver from the dishes at their stations rather than putting everything together in one tub. His idea is working so far. Jonathan saved us money, and I really appreciate that he was interested enough to take it upon himself to share an idea that has reduced our overhead and ultimately increased our profits.

The principal of an elementary school told us about a teacher who was creative about saving money:

Rhonda teaches fourth grade and wanted to provide small gifts as "rewards" for her students. There was no room in the budget, so she contacted several local businesses and asked for extra promotional items they no longer used, such as pens, pencils, rulers, tablets, and posters. Happy to help, they also donated some furniture and even a computer! Rhonda invited the other teachers to share the wealth. Now everyone is benefiting, and the money we saved was used to expand our music and arts department.

Visionary employees are tuned in to thinking about saving money while also increasing productivity. What could you do in your company that would decrease costs and offer the customer more value in products or service? Valuable employees are just as careful with the company's money as they are with their own. With this philosophy, they become an integral part of the financial success of their company. If all employees took a more active role in saving their company money, there might be fewer layoffs. Maybe the job you save will be your own. And it is an excellent way to add to your value as an employee.

CREATE AND MAINTAIN A POSITIVE, VISIBLE PRESENCE INSIDE AND OUTSIDE YOUR COMPANY

Adding value to your job will mean more to your employability if your company's decision-makers know who you are. Your presence must be felt in a positive way and linked to the contributions you personally make to your company's success. Many employees do just the opposite. They argue, whine, and complain endlessly to attract attention. But negative attention does not help anyone whose goal is to stay employed. People should associate your name, face, and expertise with positive feelings about your work and your value to the company.

A purchasing manager illustrated this point:

> There are a lot of people around here who are trying to be visible so we don't forget who they are. But they're going about it in the wrong way. For example, I dread seeing Bill walk into our staff meeting on Monday morning because I know he will manage to criticize and find fault with every idea anyone suggests. Whether he's right or wrong, he will argue his case until we've all had enough. I think he wants to make sure we know he's here, but most of the time we wish he were somewhere—anywhere—else!

Bill would have been better off staying *invisible!* The questions to ask yourself are: Do your customers, co-workers, and employer know who you are? And if they do, would a discussion about you and your work be positive and favorable? Employees who are disliked will eventually be history, of course. But firings and layoffs often occur as a result of conversations among a few people discussing the options and asking themselves: "Which employees are vital and essential to our company's continued growth?" You do want your name to come up in that discussion, as long as it is followed by positive, persuasive comments about the necessity of keeping you on board. What reaction would occur when your name is brought up for discussion?

How, then, can an employee become visible in a positive way? One CEO commented:

> We want employees working for us who are actively achieving recognition in our organization. I expect my most valuable employees to volunteer for special projects and to take their turn serving as team leaders.

Another CEO added:

Employees should be involved in professional organizations as well as community activities. That's one way I determine who is bringing value to our organization.

Unfortunately, employees often have a different attitude:

- ▣ I have enough work to do, and nobody is paying me to do all this extra stuff. I have no desire to be on a special project or head up a special committee.

- ▣ I'm paid to work until 4:30 and I work until 4:30. My company does not have the right to tell me I have to join a community organization. My personal life is my own business.

- ▣ When I get home, I want to read the paper. I don't want to have to read a professional journal or something that is going to make me a better employee. At home, I'm off duty.

- ▣ My leisure time is my own. I resent my company telling me I should spend my free time fixing up houses in old neighborhoods or helping build a company float for the town's Christmas parade.

Employees are certainly within their rights to leave at day's end, decline to serve on committees and special projects, refuse to read work-related publications, and refrain from being active in their communities. Nevertheless, these are the things employees are doing every day in every business to add value and set themselves apart from those employees who choose not to go the extra mile.

Others think: "But I'm doing all that already! I'm valuable!" Fine. But does anybody else but you know how valuable you are? Demonstrating value usually requires extra effort and a commitment to document your accomplishments and let others know that you are valuable. An engineer told us:

My boss volunteered me to be the team captain to raise funds for the Girl Scout Council in our area, and I was to coordinate the efforts of all the other engineering firms in our city. A big task, so I decided to "get visible" with my efforts. Instead of giving him a final report at the end of the campaign six weeks later, I sent him a brief memo every Friday, updating our efforts and telling him how much closer we were to reaching our goal. I also let him know that a well-known community leader made a sizable donation and was also considering our firm for a special project as the result of a personal visit from me. All this took some extra effort on my part, but I think it was well worth it.

Brandon, a mid-level sales manager, was also able to document extra value:

We initiated a "customer appreciation" week in which all our salespeople would call on their best customers and thank them for doing business with us. Two days prior to the start of the campaign, my boss was rushed to the hospital for emergency surgery. Rather than postpone our efforts for three weeks until he was back on the job, I offered to coordinate the entire project. It was a lot of extra work, in addition to my other duties, but I did a great job. When he got back to work, my boss gave me full credit for saving the project. I worked hard and made sure I got the visibility I deserved.

The time when an employee could simply come to work, do the job, and go home has passed. Now a positive attitude, commitment, vision, and top performance have become an integral part of every job. Are you creating visibility for yourself in your company? Do the people in decision-making roles know who you are and what you do that contributes to the success of your company? Your job may be at risk because no one is aware of what you do.

DOCUMENT YOUR ACCOMPLISHMENTS

In today's job market, documentation is the name of the game. Although most employees realize the importance of documenting what their subordinates and customers are doing, they are not so active in documenting their own accomplishments. In the past, they were used to having managers set job standards and evaluate them once a year during their performance review. It was up to the managers to document the employee's performance. But times have changed, and it's becoming increasingly more common for employees to be asked to convince their company why they should be kept on the payroll. An employee can provide the best answer to this question by documenting added value.

A human resource director explained how things have changed:

In the past, "documentation" meant writing down in triplicate every little thing you said and did. Although this type of tedious journal-keeping is often still necessary in instances where potential legal issues could arise, the type of documentation now being encouraged is more a "sharing of information, ideas, and strategies" with the team.

Many employees have a difficult time with such a concept because they were raised with this advice from well-meaning adults: "Don't brag. Don't be conceited. No one will like you if you boast or blow your own horn." If you got that message when you were growing up, forget it and replace it with this one: "I do some really special things for this company. I should be recognized as an employee they need to keep because of the added value I bring to my job. It is up to me to let them know how and what I contribute to the ongoing success of our company."

A marketing director explained why self-documentation is so important:

For most of our staff, self-evaluation is never easy. But identifying their strengths is a skill worth developing. Whether they feel comfortable or not, they will have to share ideas, let people know what they are doing, what their team is doing, what ideas they are working on, what type of workshops and training sessions they are attending, and anything else that will prove they are interested, excited, and committed to their job, our company, our customers, and our future together.

Documentation is especially important if your job doesn't appear to be directly linked to bottom-line financial results. Many people being laid off now are in what companies refer to as "soft jobs"—those that appear to have no direct customer contact and whose impact is difficult to measure. Unfortunately, the new trend is to eliminate jobs in human resources, personnel, training and education, and research and development—although these jobs are crucial to any company whose main goal is to provide the utmost in customer service and value.

A manager explained the importance of these "less-visible" departments in her company:

> Employees who are not educated about our products or services cannot provide the necessary benefits to our customers to sell those products and services. We also know that without careful research and ongoing development, our products will become obsolete and we will no longer be able to meet our customers' needs in the marketplace.

It may be difficult to comprehend why these jobs are often the first to go. But decision-makers tend to keep the jobs that can show profitable results on paper now. Since results in the "softer" jobs are not as easily measured, employees in these positions must look for unique, creative ways to document the value of their work and their ultimate value to the company. A human resource director of a hospital told us this story:

> For so long, no one ever asked me anything. I did whatever I wanted to do in my department and I didn't have to answer to anyone. I watched as my fellow managers would panic each month to present a monthly report and I would delight

in the fact that I did not have to be accountable to anyone. However, my CEO recently informed me that he didn't think my job is necessary. I know how many employees I've helped, and how many managers I have trained to be better leaders. But I realized I failed to keep him abreast of what I was doing. Even though a great deal of my job is confidential, I could have shared many examples of how I was saving my company money. I enjoyed the autonomy, but that is exactly what has put my job in danger.

A patient representative handled a similar situation in a different way and ultimately saved her job:

I've spent many a late night here consoling family members, handling complaints, and dealing with difficult patients, but no one really knew what I did. Then I got word my job would be cut within three months because I wasn't contributing to the bottom line. So I decided to create a patient survey. I started delivering a monthly summary, in person, to our CEO. I pointed out two potential lawsuits and the steps I took to avoid them, along with all the positive feedback from patients about how well they were treated and how they would recommend our hospital to others. I still hate reports, but now it's what I have to do to keep my job.

One important method of self-documentation is to create and maintain an updated résumé. It's always wise to keep your options open and a well-written résumé may be the best format for documenting your job history as well as your skills, talents, education, training, and all those "extras" that make you a valuable part of your organization. A professional résumé can be shared with your manager, providing a way to compare your experiences of the previous year and to show that you are constantly striving to add more training, skills, and responsibilities. List your projects, achievements, committee involvement, community volunteer work, or anything else that demonstrates your special talents and abilities. And when you are asked to document what you've accomplished, you can use your résumé as a running record.

A personnel supervisor explained:

> Like many other companies, we are using a résumé format for the annual performance appraisal review. If an employee's résumé has not been recently enhanced and updated by means of a new project, more committee involvement, or a completed course or training session, then there has been no value added. The employee has not moved beyond the previous year's accomplishments. And that leads us to question whether this employee is adding value to our company any longer.

Just as most companies compile an annual report which they send to their stockholders to show their growth and success, a résumé is a valuable way for employees to document their own success. Having a fully updated résumé on hand is excellent for another reason, too. If you should, at some point, find out that you are in danger of losing your job, you can take action immediately. Instead of going to work, crossing your fingers, and praying, "Oh, please, don't let it be me!" you can begin to explore your options and alternatives as soon as possible. You, and only you, are in charge of your career, and documentation is one of the most important ways to ensure your future employability.

CULTIVATE ADVOCATES AND ALLIES

When a group of decision-makers is seated around a conference table discussing each employee (many of whom they do not even know personally) in an attempt to determine who should stay and who should go, we asked you earlier what you thought the response would be if your name came up for discussion at that table. Now we have another, and perhaps even more important, question: who will bring your name to the attention of this group in a positive way? To stay employed you will need someone to go to bat for you. Since you will rarely be invited into those closed-door sessions which could very well determine your future, you must have an advocate (or many advocates) to speak up for you and your value to the company.

Who would be your advocate when your name comes up? Who could you count on to work with your best interests in mind? Because they cannot win the battle alone, you have a responsibility to give your advocates the ammunition they need to go to bat for you by providing them with positive and solid documentation of the value you bring to the company. Alex told us about his strongest advocate, his manager:

> Wayne knew my job was on the line. There were three of us in the department, and only two positions available. He worked for days gathering information from me and my customers about what an outstanding job I do and how well I service my clients. He went into that meeting with a folder of facts, statistics, and testimonial letters. I know he's the reason why I have my job today.

Naturally, your most important advocate is your boss, since his or her recommendation, or lack thereof, is a crucial factor in determining your job security. But many employees don't extend their network of advocates beyond their immediate supervisors. This could be a serious mistake. Angela, a print shop assistant, said:

> I was totally consumed with pleasing my boss. I figured if he liked my work, my job would be safe. But one day he was gone—fired—just like that. I realized too late that no one else in the company even knew who I was. I had opportunities to be involved in interdepartmental projects and teams, but I always said I was too busy and didn't want the extra work. That was a big mistake. Now I have no one to fight for me next week when they decide which employees to lay off.

Although you should definitely pursue your boss as an advocate, don't stop there. You must have other champions who are also committed to keeping you on the payroll. Make a list of the people you know you could count on to fight for you and your job. If your list is short, you should expand your professional relationships. Champions can be found in all departments, branches, divisions, and teams. Get to know as many people as possible within all areas of your company, as well as your community. You never know who might be in a position one day to fight for you. A newly promoted manager told us this story:

> Bryce and I had worked together for years. I always tried to be friendly, share information, and help him when he needed it. But he never reciprocated. Instead, he took full credit for projects we completed together, failed to give me messages, and turned some of my customers against me so he could add them to his accounts list. Last week, I was promoted to head of our department and my first task was to lay off two of our eight employees. When the CEO asked my feelings about each employee's strengths and weaknesses, I had to be honest. Bryce is not a positive team player, and he has to go.

This story is really not as far-fetched as it may appear. In any company, the people you work alongside today could be the ones you report to tomorrow. Never miss the opportunity to make an ally, even if you don't perceive that person to be in a position of power. This is the time to make allies of as many people as possible. It is not the time to be a loner, because it could very well be *other* people who will decide your future with this company.

Now sit down, take a deep breath, and ask yourself what you have done to:

- Help your company make money;
- Help your company save money;
- Create and maintain a positive, visible presence inside and outside your company;
- Document your accomplishments; and
- Cultivate advocates and allies.

Once you have the answers to these questions, you will have a much better understanding of how you could answer the all-important question that will be asked of you one day in the near future: *"What added value do you bring to your job that contributes directly to the financial stability, success, and growth of our company?"*

CHAPTER 3

Have a Positive Impact on Your Company, Customers, and Colleagues

▣ Which employees would I keep? The ones who are determined to set a positive tone through their performance and behavior. I can teach my employees how to do the job. I can provide in-service training to update their skills. But I cannot mentor, teach, or coach them to have a positive attitude.

This same sentiment was expressed over and over again by CEOs, human resource directors, managers, and business owners. Every one of them was adamant about the importance of employees having a positive attitude. But when they attempted to define a positive attitude, they found it was difficult to put into words what they meant.

"Oh, great!" an employee might say. "Just how am I supposed to improve a quality like 'attitude' when no one can even tell me what it means?" Perhaps attitude is best defined as "a state of mind." And that state of mind is revealed by our behavior. That's why most of us tend to use words like "happy" and "enjoyable to be around" when we try to describe a person with a positive attitude. Our attitude affects our behavior, which, in turn, is demonstrated by our performance. No wonder attitude is so important in the business world. It determines how we do our jobs.

Some employees resist this notion. "No one has the right to tell me how to think," they may say. Employers do not have the right to evaluate our inner thoughts and feelings. But they do have the right to evaluate how we behave as a result of those thoughts and feelings.

Employers and companies also have the right to expect that an employee's behavior and performance will have a positive impact upon their organizations. An employee can have a positive or negative impact on a company. And all would agree that an organization comprised of employees who have a negative influence on their customers and co-workers will not be in business for very long. Organizations whose employees have a positive impact on their co-workers, their customers, and their company will stay in business.

Sometimes positive behavior does not accurately reflect someone's internal attitude. In other words, you can feel any way you want: sad, depressed, lonely, angry, even apathetic—as long as you don't act that way at work. No employer can require you to change or adjust your beliefs, feelings, or perceptions. Those belong to you. But to keep your job, you will have to commit to behaving in ways that will be seen by others as having a positive impact upon the organization. And what are those behaviors? To find out, we began by asking employers to describe an employee who had a positive impact on their companies:

▣ Sally is always thinking about what to do next. She loves to figure out new ways to improve our service and please our customers.

▣ Ron never complains. If there is a problem, he immediately comes up with several alternate options that might work.

▣ Karen enjoys people. She is always willing to pitch in and help, even if it's not really her specific job.

◉ Michael has had a rough life and lots of family issues. He never uses his problems as an excuse to stop him from getting the job done.

◉ Sara always takes responsibility instead of blaming other people or other departments. She sets about fixing the problem instead of finding fault.

Time and time again, employers described employees who were visionary *(she looks ahead)*, proactive *(he doesn't use his problems as an excuse)*, problem-solvers *(never complains, always has options)*, and people-centered *(enjoys people, always willing to help)*. These seemed to be the behaviors that employers were looking for when determining who was "positive" and who was not. It was wonderful to see how excited they were when they talked about these employees. Would your employer be enthusiastic when describing your performance to another person? If your employability depends upon it, it's certainly something to consider.

An executive vice president with a large insurance company had no trouble describing an employee he felt had a positive impact upon his organization:

Pat is a problem-solver and a motivator who can identify a problem and determine, "We have to get this done. What's the best way to start?" No matter what happened in our company—downsizing, layoffs, whatever—I would not let Pat go. I would hunt until I found her a job, even if it was another position. There is no way I would let a person with her drive for excellence and dedication to our company and our customers go to another company. We could not afford to let our competition get hold of her. In a time when our company's assets are our primary concern, Pat is one of our most valuable assets.

At this point, some employees may ask: "How can I separate my attitude from my actions? This is just who I am." Rest assured, it's done every day. Employees constantly find themselves in situations where they simply cannot let their internal feelings influence their actions. Put yourself in these situations. Would you like your surgeon to be all thumbs because he was upset with his wife? Or a fireman to drive slowly when you called in an alarm because he was a bit tired? Or your lawyer to argue your case poorly because she didn't feel like talking today? Or the lifeguard to daydream about getting a new job out of the sun instead of paying attention while your child was swimming? These people are required to behave in a certain, prescribed way regardless of their attitude. And we certainly expect them to do that—no matter what.

On a recent visit to Disney World, I (Connie) encountered an employee who exemplified this concept. Observing Mickey Mouse giving his fans his undivided attention, I realized I was watching "the consummate professional" in action. He was courteous, energetic, enthusiastic, and eager to please everyone, even though he must have been hot and uncomfortable in that heavy, bulky costume, poked and prodded by children who were pulling on his arms and legs, eager to spend a moment with their hero. He had probably been at this for hours, yet he continued to play the part of Mickey Mouse—happy, friendly, and accommodating.

Like Mickey, we all play a part. And our customers, whether we call them clients, members, patients, students, or guests, expect us to play our parts well—regardless of whatever else is going on in our personal and professional lives. While your company should not expect you to behave in a way that is unethical or takes away from who you are, it does have the right to expect you to play the part of a professional, even when you're not feeling particularly enthusiastic, compassionate, or whatever it is your job requires you to be.

But how do you stay enthusiastic and excited about your job if you've been at it for quite a while and things at work or at home are not going perfectly? Remember, when actors are on stage, they know they must be so good at what they do that their performance will set them apart from the rest of the cast and make them memorable. No matter how famous and successful an actor may be, he or she is always aware of an understudy waiting in the wings, eager to take over the role the moment that actor begins to deliver a performance which is less than top quality. In today's world of downsizing and layoffs, we all have understudies—people who would love to take our place and play the part the job requires. To remain employable, you must make sure you are one of your company's "star performers." Your customers also have the right to a star performance because they are your audience. That's really what your paycheck is: a reward for playing your part well. Can your organization count on you, as a professional, to be a star performer?

That doesn't mean you should be phony or just go through the mechanical motions of acting out your part. Listen to this CEO:

> I don't want an officeful of robots, but I also don't want people who bring their negative feelings to work every day. Think of what a different workplace we could create if everyone came to work and focused on the job at hand, instead of allowing our internal attitudes to affect our performance.

Because we're human, we have a tendency to wish that things were perfect, and that everything in our personal and professional lives would run smoothly all the time. No matter how hard we try, life will never be perfect, but as professionals we are paid to perform in spite of everyday trials and tribulations. Unfortunately, there are employees in every organization who lapse into complaining every time something goes wrong. Perhaps a co-worker made a mistake, or they've had to deal with a difficult and demanding customer. Although complaining is a natural tendency for some people, it has a negative cumulative effect on everyone else's mood. A negative attitude can be just as contagious as a positive one. One person starts complaining: "We're working long hours . . . we don't have enough help . . . there's too much pressure . . . nobody appreciates us . . ." and pretty soon, several other people have joined "the pity party." From that point on, a gray cloud has settled which can dampen enthusiasm and diminish the performance of others on the team.

In contrast, we all know how much we enjoy being around a co-worker who is not only smart and on top of the job, but upbeat and positive as well—no matter what the circumstances. I (Connie) recently met an airline employee who was able to do just that. My plane was late and I ran for the last connection home, only to discover the flight was delayed for two hours. Spotting an agent coming toward me, I got ready to let him know I was not happy. But before I could begin, another passenger stepped in front of me and took the words right out of my mouth. But he was far more *vocal*. In fact, he was rude and obnoxious. He yelled, swore, and shook his finger in the agent's face. The agent was amazing—cool, calm, and courteous. He responded to each insult with an apology and an offer to help. At one point, he even said, "I understand this has been a very disappointing and frustrating day for you. We'll work this out." Slowly the man calmed down and began to work with the agent to solve his problem. After he walked away, fairly mollified, the agent turned to me and politely said, "I'm sorry to have kept you waiting. How may I help you?"

I tried to remember how angry I had been, but I simply said, "You were great!"

"What?" he asked, with a puzzled look.

"You were great. You handled that situation perfectly!" Then I noticed how exhausted he looked and suddenly I realized how many tired, angry people he had been dealing with in the last half hour. "I'll bet this is not exactly how you planned to spend your evening, is it?" I asked.

A look of surprise crossed his face, and he answered, "As a matter of fact—no, it isn't. My shift ended two hours ago, but with all the delays I had to stay late. Tonight is open house at my son's school, and he was so excited about my coming and meeting his teachers. Now my son is angry with me. My wife is angry with me, too, and every passenger on your flight is angry with me. No, this isn't exactly what I had planned for tonight."

"Well, you certainly don't act like you're upset," I replied. "You've been so polite, so helpful, and so professional."

He turned to me and said, matter-of-factly, "But that's my job. Being polite and helpful and solving problems, being professional even when I don't feel like it—that's my job. That's what they count on me to do, whether I feel like it or not."

Polite, helpful, and professional—that was how that agent described his job. He did not tell me his job was collecting tickets or rerouting passengers or scheduling flights. His job was to be polite, helpful, and professional. How about you? How would you describe your job?

Realistically, we all know that a positive attitude is not the answer to everything, and it doesn't solve all of a company's problems. As one human resource director put it:

I guess every company has a few employees with a positive attitude and a sunny disposition who are also incompetent, lazy, disorganized, and unwilling to deal with change. Having a "positive attitude" means more than just putting on "a happy face." It means having the energy, motivation, and desire to treat your customers and co-workers respectfully and professionally.

From your own experience, think about how you feel when you have to work with a negative person. Do you remember times when someone else's negativity influenced your own performance that day? Even though you may love your job and you're proud of the products and services you deliver, you probably felt that you and your company weren't doing their best. Margaux, a computer analyst, told us about a discouraging situation in her workplace:

I tried to get away from a negative co-worker by transferring to another department. Wouldn't you know it? Six months later she applied for a transfer into my department and I was right back where I started. I am so miserable! My only choices now are to endure her or escape totally by quitting. With three kids to feed and clothe, I don't have that luxury.

Most people can identify with Margaux because they cannot quit their jobs. But if you do have to work with negative people, try to limit additional interaction. You are not obligated to carpool with them, go to lunch with them, or spend time with them after work. Part of your responsibility as a professional is to be the kind of employee that others are not trying to get away from, but rather, to be a positive person with whom they enjoy working.

A new attitude now prevails among company owners, managers, supervisors, co-workers, and customers, and it looks as if the trend will continue to build into the next decade and the next century. Everyone we interviewed was fed up with negative attitudes and poor performance. And they were certainly tired of dealing with employees who only know one phrase: *"That's not my job."* Employers today are looking for people who are excited and positive about working for their company. But employers don't always get what they expect. The human resource manager at a large hospital told us:

> We owe our employees a safe environment, safe working conditions, and challenging work. But what do they owe us in return? We have some employees in our company who haven't figured out it's a two-way street. They take, take, take . . . and never deliver what they're being paid to do. But we're not worried, because after this downsizing, they won't be around anymore.

The CEO of a small community bank had a strong opinion about employees who don't give their best to the job:

> When an employee comes to work and doesn't give me 100 percent of his or her energy and ability, I let it slide once or twice. Then I have to decide if this is the kind of person I really want—or need—on my team.

The personnel director of a mid-size insurance company explained how one employee was having a negative effect on the entire team:

We have an employee who walks around with a little gray cloud over her head. We've tried to help her, but every time we ask what's wrong, she says, "Oh, nothing!" She's beginning to affect morale. We can't afford to have anyone around who is going to demoralize and demotivate us. Talking with her hasn't worked, so we're going to have to decide how much longer we can run the risk of keeping her on board.

CEOs today are looking for employees who have a positive impact and influence on customers and co-workers. And with two thousand to three thousand people losing their jobs every day, now might not be the best time to be perceived as having a negative impact upon your company. But if you're going to become a positive influence on others, you must take time to evaluate your interactions and their effects. Both verbal and nonverbal communication are important. What you say must match what you do. One manager commented:

I strongly encourage the people on my team to spend some time answering questions like this: Do you focus on the positive aspects of your job? Are you willing to work together as part of a team? Is your conversation upbeat and positive? Do you compliment others when they do a good job? The answers to these questions are important because I can't afford to have negative people around who will make me and my department look bad.

How would you answer the above questions if your manager posed them to you? Are you recognized as one of the most positive people in your department and in your company? If not, what are you willing to do about it?

Almost everyone we interviewed talked about the importance of employees who were not only *positive* but also *proactive*—who take control of their own lives instead of trying to control others or allowing others to control them. As one CEO put it:

We need proactive people who will take full responsibility for their successes and their shortcomings, instead of reacting to people and situations around them. Our company can only be as proactive as the people on our payroll.

Would you consider yourself a proactive person? Would your CEO and your manager describe your behavior as proactive or reactive? As another CEO added, perplexed:

Reactive people stand out like sore thumbs. They spend so much time complaining and reacting to the problems around them that they have no time or energy to solve those problems. I can spend an hour observing new employees and know whether they will be a proactive asset or a reactive liability to our company. And if they're a liability, they won't be here too long.

The human resource director of a major manufacturing company gave us this example of how two of his employees handled the same situation in different ways. At a recent team meeting, Janet and David were told that their department had fallen behind schedule due to some unforeseen problems which affected their ability to get a project completed on time. Their team leader asked for everyone's cooperation in working one extra hour every day for two weeks to get the project back on track. Otherwise, their company would lose a very important contract with one of its best customers.

Although she wasn't happy about it, Janet immediately began working on a plan to make sure she could do her part. "I'll have to ask one of the other mothers to pick up the kids from school and drop them off at home. I'll have to arrange for a sitter, and my husband will have to start dinner, since he'll get home before I do. It will be tough, but it will be worth it."

On the other hand, David spent all his time complaining and his co-workers had no choice but to listen. "This is not fair! This is not the job I bargained for. And it's not even my fault. I wasn't even here when all this happened! I've been on vacation for two weeks. Now I'm going to be all stressed out over something that's not even my fault or my problem."

Do you see the difference? David spent his time and energy whining and complaining while Janet spent her time and energy helping to solve the problem. So what's the lesson learned here? This CEO went on to say that, two months later, when some cutbacks in staff needed to be made, it was no surprise to him—or anyone else in the company—that David was laid off and Janet kept her job. In fact, the only one surprised at this turn of events was David! Many employees spend their time complaining, griping, and reacting negatively, and then are astounded when they're the first to go.

You may not realize it, but your performance has the power to make or break your organization. Your attitude can be your greatest asset or your greatest liability. Unaware of that, employees have said to us: "My job is hard work! And my company doesn't even try to motivate me to do my best." In fact, today's companies realize that it is not their responsibility to motivate employees because motivation cannot come from the outside. Motivation is "an inside job." This means that employees should not have to be coddled or coerced into working hard and doing an excellent job. A valuable employee, the kind a company would work hard to hire and retain, is self-motivated.

Today's employers are looking for employees who:

- Want to work;
- Enjoy what they do;
- Take pride in their company, their products, and their services;
- Care about their customers and their co-workers;
- Are the kind of team player others like to be around;
- Make work a better place by their good humor, dependability, integrity, and their ability to be a positive influence through their words and actions.

This is what the companies of the future will expect from you. Over and over, CEOs, human resource directors, managers, and employers confirmed that the attitude of one person is contagious.

If attitude is contagious, is yours worth catching? Is your attitude helping to create a healthy environment in your organization? What can you do—and what do you need to do—to stand out from the rest and be easily recognized as an employee who has a positive influence on your customers, your colleagues, and your company? How are you being perceived by the people who make the decisions that can—and will—affect your future? To stay employed, you have to love your job and play your part well.

CHAPTER 4

Embrace and Initiate Change

▣ Which employees would I keep? The ones who can adapt to all of the changes our company is going through with professionalism, determination, and optimism. We need employees who are resilient enough to face change boldly, without resorting to complaining, apathy, anger, or fear.

CEOs, managers, human resource directors, and business owners today feel strongly about the need to have employees who are successful change agents for their team and their company as a whole. What do we mean by the term "change agent"? An agent is someone who represents the interests of another person or company, and his or her job is to take care of business and make sure everything goes smoothly. Thus, a change agent helps take care of an employer's business by facilitating change.

Are you a change agent for your company? Can others count on you to make sure things go smoothly? Do you continue to take care of business in the midst of change? One CEO expressed his frustration with the varying degrees of adaptability among his employees:

Some employees love change and some hate it. Some welcome it and some fear it. While some employees are asking, "What took it so long to get here?" others try to close their eyes and hope it will go away. Many are coming to work enthusiastic and excited about being part of the "new" company, but just as many are acting afraid, unsure, and apathetic.

Because change is an integral part of today's business climate, it is surprising that so many people make such a big deal about it. One CEO told us:

We plan to schedule six staff meetings this quarter, and three of them will focus on change issues. We already have our titles: "Surviving Change," "Dealing with the Stress of Change," and "Change Doesn't Have to Kill You."

No wonder some people are afraid of change! With titles like that, who wouldn't be afraid? Although some employees have been conditioned to fear change, we mustn't lose sight of the fact that change is normal. In fact, it's always been normal. We sometimes forget just how resilient people really are. We have conquered new worlds, fought plagues and disease, adapted to new cultures, and integrated new inventions that transformed our lives. We've moved from the age of agriculture to the industry age and, now, to the information age. Humanity has evolved because we are masters of change.

Why do we automatically assume that we cannot continue to integrate change successfully in our lives? We are better educated, healthier, and more mobile than any other generation. We should be able to handle change just as well as (or even better than) our ancestors. Imagine the Pilgrims aboard the *Mayflower* being required to attend workshops about dealing with the changes of relocating to a brand-new country without homes, schools, churches, and stores. They didn't read self-help books on the strategies for coping with stress, or form support groups to work out their inner feelings about living in close quarters with strangers for three to four months during the voyage to the New World. They simply decided what they wanted to do—and they did it!

A human resource director expressed her concern that some companies are sending the wrong message to their employees about change, and that's why there are problems:

> Somewhere along the line, we got the message that we might not survive the change experience—that we couldn't deal with it—and that change might not be good for us. While it's true that change isn't easy, we must believe we can, indeed, survive it and that it will only harm us if we let it. Perhaps we don't give people enough credit. Maybe everyone can handle change if we approach it like we have in the past—with determination, hard work, concentrated effort, and a good sense of humor.

Most of us will experience unpredictable and sometimes painful changes in our personal lives. And to the greatest extent possible, we should not permit those changes to intrude upon our professional lives. But changes in the workplace are another matter. They can occur as a result of new thinking, advances in technology, innovation and progress, knowledge and communication, as well as mergers, takeovers, layoffs, and downsizing. These organizational changes can directly affect our professional lives and, ultimately, our personal lives. They may also lead to feelings of sadness, frustration, grief, and anger, especially when jobs are lost or worse, when an entire company ceases to exist. So let's talk about how we can make this normal life experience—change—as positive and beneficial as possible.

One CEO noted the two distinctly different ways her employees are dealing with change:

> We've been in the midst of major reorganizational change for the past two years. Our staff seems to be divided into two distinct groups. The first group is concentrating on finding new ideas and new processes that can take them and their departments to a higher level of expertise. They are learning from every person they meet and every experience they have. Some of them are going back to school to increase their

knowledge base, sharpen their skills, and make themselves more valuable to our company.

The second group is not open to new ideas and processes, and they constantly talk about a return to "the good old days." Wishing, hoping, worrying, and crossing their fingers won't keep them employed. And without a doubt, my managers and I are relying more and more on the people in the first group. We're trying to avoid layoffs, but if it comes to that, there is no doubt which group we would keep.

Do groups like this exist in your workplace? If so, in which group do you find yourself? How would your CEO describe your approach to change?

Change is here to stay, and it's happening faster than ever before. It's been said that we have more printed information now in a Sunday edition of the *New York Times* than our grandparents had in their entire lifetime. Thinking that change will eventually cease, and being unprepared for the changes that are already underway, will make our lives a lot more difficult. Change requires a great deal of emotional creativity and energy if it is to have a positive impact on our lives. The branch manager of a bank summed it up perfectly:

Some of our employees are wasting so much emotional energy hanging on to old habits and beliefs that there is no energy left in them to tackle the changes we're facing in the banking industry. That negative attitude affects their fellow co-workers, but it also clouds their decision-making ability and hurts their chances for future success with the organization.

Companies want employees who can face these new challenges with a positive outlook. One manager of a credit union told her employees at a staff meeting:

We know change can sometimes appear frightening and intimidating. But change can also be very rewarding. If you don't push yourself to the limit, you will never know how far you can really go.

Like it or not, changes in our personal and professional lives often occur so rapidly that there is little or no time to adapt or adjust to the current one before another one comes along. Any woman who has been through childbirth can remember when she first experienced labor pains. We said to ourselves, "What's the big deal? This will be easy!" But as the labor progressed, many of us changed our minds! Going through change is a lot like experiencing labor pains. It wouldn't be a problem if we had time in between—time to relax, calm down, adjust, and get ready for the next one. Unfortunately, we don't often have that luxury with the rapid pace of today's changes.

Even if the pains of change are coming one right after another and we don't always have time to adjust, we do have the power to choose how we react. We can scream, yell at everyone around us, and blame others, or we can take a deep breath and work with the process. As you evaluate these choices, keep one thing in mind. The more we fight and tense up, the more painful the changes will be. Resisting never kept a baby from being born, and it won't keep a new idea from taking hold. Resisting simply makes the process longer and more painful. Change will happen—no matter what. We will handle it better when we learn to breathe, to relax, and to move with the change—not against it.

This is definitely not the time to drag your feet because managers are not inclined to take employees by the hand and lead them through the change process. A supervisor from a water treatment plant stated it perfectly when he said:

> Some of our folks tell me they're willing to change, as long as they can do it at their own speed. They don't see themselves as resisting change—they just want to take their own sweet time. They call it "adjusting at their own pace." I call it failing to cooperate for the good of the company.

Stalling for time and resisting change can have a negative impact on your customers, your co-workers, and your company. To be successful, the entire team must pull together. Sometimes employees say they don't believe their reluctance to embrace change will even be noticed because they see themselves as only a small spoke in a very large corporate wheel. But managers and CEOs do, indeed, notice. The managing partner of a large law firm commented:

When I was a kid back in the mid-1950s, we were the only family on the block who didn't have a TV set because my dad said television was a whim—a fad that would never last. Some of our partners remind me of my dad. They refuse to accept the fact that we must computerize our research. We no longer have the time to spend hours researching cases, and we're spending too much money hiring people to do it for us. The resistance of a few is negatively impacting the entire firm.

Other managers made similar comments, confirming the fact that they do notice when an employee is reluctant to change. This does not mean, however, that we should automatically go along with every new idea that comes up. It also does not mean that an employee cannot express an opinion or disagree with suggested changes. The manager of a large grocery store chain told us:

We appreciate employees who are not afraid to stand up for what they believe is best for our customer and our company. They don't gripe and complain about new changes, but give us such professional and insightful information that we are willing to listen and reconsider our direction.

People are uncertain about how to react to change. One employee said, "I'm confused. Just what does my company want? If I say something about the change, I'll be seen as a complainer. Yet if I don't say anything, I may be viewed as being unassertive and unwilling to stand up for my beliefs." In this kind of dilemma, employees must carefully evaluate each situation and do what is right at that moment. They must be able to analyze and explain their reasons for fighting for or against a change. It's best to save your arguments against change for the times when you feel so strongly that you have little choice but to speak out. But it's also important to recognize when a decision to change has been made and no amount of opposition or discussion will alter that course.

CEOs and managers want commitment to change when it is necessary. Knowing that, then, why are so many people resistant to it? The number one reason is fear, although very few people are willing to admit it. None of us want to acknowledge that we doubt our ability to integrate new ideas, use new technology, or adapt to new organizations. We don't even want to think about what's ahead: new management, new ways of doing things, new terminology, new titles, and new job descriptions. Fear can have several components:

1. **Fear of the unknown:** What will happen to my company, my job, my life, as I know it now? How secure is my future?

2. **Fear of not being in control:** What should I do? Should I just wait around while they make decisions that could seriously affect my life?

3. **Fear of being inadequate:** I know how to do this job now, but will I be able to do it as well as they expect me to when everything has changed? And if I can't, what happens then?

4. **Fear of moving outside our personal comfort zone:** I've been doing my job this way for years, and I'm very good at it. Why do we have to change what has worked so well for so long?

There is no doubt that employees often view change from a different perspective than their supervisors, managers, or CEOs. Picture the following scenario. Joe (the employee) is good at his job, works hard, and recently received a promotion. He is proud of his work and considers himself a valuable employee. Content with his salary and benefits, Joe plans to continue at this job until he retires. Today the CEO of his company has called an emergency meeting. Notice Joe's thoughts (in italics) as the meeting progresses and see if you can identify the components of his fear.

The CEO begins: "In the next few months, we will be implementing some exciting changes. (*Changes? What changes? What's wrong with the way we're doing things now?*) We've listened to all your ideas. (*My ideas? I don't remember anyone asking for my ideas!*) But we all need to pull together and work as a team. (*You mean work with everyone else? How will anyone know what I'm contributing? Besides, I really don't like most of these people all that much. I'm really happier working alone.*) We're going to be eliminating some of the middle management positions so we can have better communication from the bottom up. (*That figures! I spent years working for this promotion and now it may be history.*) We'll be eliminating our titles and simply referring to each other as team members and team players. (*I love my title! Don't take my title. I worked so hard to earn it!*) We need to improve quality and cut costs. (*That means we have to work harder and longer for the same pay.*) We need to become lean. (*That means more jobs will be cut.*) We're counting on your enthusiastic help. (*More work for the same pay and you want me to be enthusiastic?*) And we don't want you to worry. (*What do you mean "not worry"? I have a family to take care of, bills to pay, and you're telling me I may be out of a job!*) We need your support throughout this period of change . . . (*Sure! That means you want me to work hard right up until the day I get fired.*) . . . because we're all in this together. (*That's what Indiana Jones said in the snake pit.*)"

Many employees experience some of these same fears when confronted with change and feel that management doesn't understand their side of the story. CEOs and managers often feel that it is the employees who don't understand, as evidenced by comments from this CEO:

Our staff thinks senior management has nothing better to do than sit around and think up new ways to change. We're trying to respond to outside forces and stay ahead of the competition. Our marketplace has shifted. Our customers are more demanding than ever. We don't have a choice. This company can change or it can die. And if it dies, our employees will be unemployed, and they will blame us for making the wrong choices.

It's been said that lack of communication is the number one reason why personal relationships can develop problems, and the same holds true for relationships between employers and employees. Change will require open communication on both sides. But unfortunately, fear has the power to freeze employees in their tracks and prevent them from expressing their ideas and opinions. When faced with change, we must always ask ourselves this important question: Does my resistance to change have anything to do with my own fears? That's a tough question and one that is not easy to answer honestly. It is natural to fear the unknown and lack of control. We know that we won't be quite as proficient at our tasks while we're in the process of learning to do things a new way. We know we will have to work a lot harder. Are we willing to let go of the present to embrace the future? We may not know what the future will bring, but we are responsible for what we bring to the future.

Often, a change in attitude can work wonders. When I (Jean) had finished a presentation, a woman asked if she could stay and talk. A mid-level manager at a savings and loan for eighteen years, Adrianne had been called into her supervisor's office that same week and counseled about her negative attitude regarding her changing role. "I knew I didn't like all the changes that were happening in the company, but I didn't realize my attitude was so noticeable," she told me. "I thought change was all fine and good, until it began to personally affect the way I do my job. First, I had to give up my office and I was relocated to a cubicle. That was a hard pill to swallow. Then I was assigned two job responsibilities, tasks I had performed years ago when I was a brand-new receptionist: opening safe deposit boxes and giving out tokens so customers could get out of our parking lot. Now I felt like I was moving backward instead of forward."

I suggested a subtle change in Adrianne's attitude. Instead of thinking, "I can't believe someone with my seniority is being asked to perform such lowly tasks," she could say to herself: "I can't believe I'm being so well compensated to give out parking lot tokens and open safe deposit boxes!" Adrianne laughed and said, "I'll try it! That does sound a lot more positive than the way I was looking at it."

Adrianne began to display a more positive attitude when she decided to ask senior management if she could schedule weekly meetings within her own department to bring her co-workers together to talk about their questions and concerns regarding upcoming changes. Senior management was so impressed with this idea that they instituted weekly departmental change meetings throughout the entire organization. In fact, they asked Adrianne to coordinate and run the meetings in conjunction with the education and training department. (Remember, in this age of downsizing, when you suggest a new idea, you might become the person in charge of implementing it.)

When I saw Adrianne again a few months later and asked how her job was going, I was quite surprised when she told me about the change meetings. "I love running those meetings," she said. "I've never done anything like this before, and it's really been fun—although it's hard work. This has been a new challenge and I'm really excited to be contributing in an important way. I see now that I was comfortable with my job, but it was getting boring. Even though I resisted change and didn't want additional work, I have to admit that it's really been fun to do something totally different than I've ever done before. In fact, I'm more excited about my job than I can ever remember."

We spoke to many employees who commented on how "tired" they were. Yet as we questioned them further, we found they were not physically tired. They were still working the same number of hours they had worked in the past. The problem was that many of them were bored. Like Adrianne, they described their jobs as boring, mundane, menial. Perhaps one of the most positive aspects of change is that it is never boring. On the contrary, it can create passion. And passion—and the excitement, creativity, and energy which accompany it—is the spark that keeps us going.

Passion could be called the charge for our life's batteries! Without that charge, it's hard to get our engines revved up. That igniting charge is sparked by the challenge of change—learning new things, meeting new people, growing as professionals, and taking risks that push us to reach our potential. None of that can happen unless and until we are willing to experience the fear that inevitably arises when we move out of our comfort zones. No risk, no fear; no fear, no passion; no passion, no fun.

If we want passion back in our lives, we must be willing to meet the challenge of change. What might that mean for you? Perhaps it might involve going back to school, learning how to work with a computer, working with a team, taking on new responsibilities, or redefining a career path. If you want to remain employable, you may have to change more than just your attitude and your reaction to change. You may have to change some of your ideas and goals to create a better future for yourself.

Even though many CEOs, human resource directors, managers, and employers spoke of their frustration with employees who resist change, there were just as many who were delighted to share stories about employees who were excited and upbeat about the changes in their jobs and their companies. Many CEOs talked about employees who were passionate about their jobs. The manager of a large retail store told us about Mike, who recently came to him and asked how he could get more involved in the change process:

> Seeing what was happening in other areas of the company, Mike realized his department was out of step with the times. Instead of pretending he didn't notice and continuing to operate in the same old way, he asked how he could help facilitate change in his department so they could get up to speed with everyone else.

A partner/owner of an office supply store told us about having to drastically cut back her staff. But there was one person she could not do without:

Janet has spent the last six months updating her skills and developing new competencies. She has asked for more responsibility, and she's always willing to take on new tasks.

Although her job title remained the same, Janet was sharp enough to know that her duties were changing, and she had to keep pace with those changes. She realized this was the time to ask for more responsibility instead of griping and complaining about what had to be done. What about you? Are you busy updating your skills? Or do you waste your time—and everyone else's—griping and complaining about change?

The CEO of a mid-size outpatient clinic told us that a group of his employees started getting together informally after work to talk about how to handle the stress involved with change:

> They shared ideas on the benefits of exercise, a healthy diet, hobbies, and outside interests, and how to keep their sense of humor in stressful times. We're excited about the outcome. As a result, they've all become closer to each other and they're working more effectively as a team in all areas.

Here is one group of employees who looked at the positive side, saw the rewards and opportunities in change, and were brought closer together by their efforts to help each other through the change process. Are there opportunities in your workplace to network, to make new friends, to interact with other departments to help each other deal with change? Could you be the catalyst in your company to start such a networking group? Are you willing to try?

All the managers we interviewed agreed that some of their most valued employees are those who can give them the honest input they need to make the best decisions regarding impending changes. The supervisor of a construction company told us how he relies on one of his best employees:

> Jeff really listens to what our customers say they like—and don't like—about doing business with us. He thinks like a cus-

tomer and he knows that the quality of our work is only as good as the customer says it is. He keeps me updated on what changes we should consider to better serve our customers.

By constantly getting feedback from customers on the job site, Jeff kept himself and his work crew from getting tunnel vision and focusing on their own needs instead of the customer's needs. How about you? Can your manager count on you for honest feedback about how change will affect your customers? Are you hindered by tunnel vision? Are you so focused on how change is affecting you that you've lost sight of what's best for your customer, your co-workers, and your company?

Obviously, there is lots of "good news" about how employees are dealing with change. Even with all the uncertainty facing them, most employees are doing a good job of handling change. Many managers and CEOs told us how proud they were of their employees who are doing whatever they can to make change work. What would your CEO, supervisor, or department manager say about your response to the changes happening in your workplace? Is there "good news" to spread about how you're handling change?

Many people are content to live their lives by playing it safe. If fear, pain, and hard work are prerequisites of change, it's easier to understand why some people are so dedicated to resisting it. They might be good at giving all the best-sounding reasons why this particular change is not right for the department, the organization, the team, or the customer. However, their underlying concern may be their fear about how the change will affect them—their job—their lives.

If you've been reacting negatively to change, it is important to modify your attitude and your behavior before it's too late. Think about what you really want. Comfort at all costs? The status quo? The good old days? If you do—if that's what you're waiting for— then you will probably soon be out of a job. If, instead, you want challenge and welcome change, you will always be employable. Try out this statement and see how it fits with your perspective on dealing with change:

◉ I accept that constant change is simply a part of life. I am continually exploring new ideas, new directions, new philosophies, new technologies, and new ways of thinking about my future. I am working to incorporate these ideas into my personal and professional life.

If this statement honestly reflects your attitude toward change, you will be a valuable employee—whatever your line of work or level of responsibility—now and long into the future.

CHAPTER 5

Work Smarter, Harder, Faster, and Better

▣ Which employee would I keep? Why, of course, the one who can get a quality job done—on time. I need employees who aren't afraid of hard work, who can be counted on to do the job right, and who don't need constant reminders or supervision. They know what needs to be done and they do it—it's as simple as that.

We have already spoken of the absolute necessity to increase productivity and work harder to avoid the alternatives: cutting staff, reducing wages and benefits, or decreasing the quality of products and/or services. There is no doubt that your employability will depend upon your determination to work as diligently as possible using the staff and resources available. Employers today are especially concerned about employees who are not working to the best of their ability. Trevor, the manager of a research facility, told us:

There is so much wasted time. Employees come in late and leave early. They take long breaks and then slowly get back to the job, stopping to talk to everyone on their way. Personal phone calls are out of hand. They plan their social life, call to buy theater tickets, and fight with their teenagers on the phone on our time. Meetings go on and on without accomplishing anything because everyone argues and can't agree on anything. We could easily handle the cutbacks we are facing if everyone would just make up their minds to come to work and work! After all, that's what they are being paid to do.

Trevor is 100 percent right. Employees should—and must—work.

We are always astonished when we hear complaints like this: "You just won't believe how hard I work. Why, I hardly have time to sit down. Work, work, work, that's all I do from the time I get to the office until the time I leave." If you've ever had those feelings yourself, it's time to face one unavoidable fact: that's why it's called work! If you're being paid within the guidelines of your job description for working reasonable hours, then your company has a right to insist that you work hard—except for lunch and brief breaks—from the time you enter the workplace until the time you leave.

Most of us are familiar with the phrase "an honest day's pay for an honest day's work." Never has an old adage been more true. This is certainly not the time to demonstrate poor work habits—especially when so many companies are evaluating who should stay and who should go. Sometimes the security of a job with sick leave, paid vacation, and co-workers who can pick up the slack when someone is having a "bad day" lulls employees into thinking that their jobs will always be there. But this is no longer the case.

As we have said before, never forget that entitlement is out and pay for performance is in. People who freelance, consult, or are self-employed know firsthand that if they do not perform to the satisfaction of their clients or customers, they will not be paid. Employees must remember that vacations, benefits, sick days, and personal days are privileges that many people do not have. But they are also part of their overall pay package and, like a salary, are earned by performing well.

Unfortunately, there are some employees who feel "entitled" to pay even if their performance is mediocre or less than satisfactory. Most CEOs and managers are frustrated with employees who feel they are owed a full day's wages for less than a full day's work. Arthur, the owner of a health club, told us:

> I have employees who feel they not only should be paid when they're sick, but also when they're tired, when they're unhappy, and when they just don't feel like working. I understand they have a right to a private life, but they forget I'm paying for the time they spend taking care of personal problems at work. I cannot continue to do that and run this company at a profit.

Another CEO had a similar point of view, along with a plan of action:

> Our company is small, and we are seriously thinking of going back to hourly wages with a time clock rather than weekly salaries. Our employees think nothing of using paid work time for phone calls, talking about their weekend plans, their diets, or their difficult spouse. With hourly wages, when they work, they get paid. When they choose not to work, they don't get paid. We still want to provide for emergencies, sick leave, and maternity leave, but other than that, we need to pay for performance and results.

Several top executives of a utility company were discussing the pay-for-performance issue as it applies to marginal employees, those who do not work to maximum capacity. They agreed that there are only two reasons why employees do not perform at the peak of their potential:

1. They are unable to do the job. They do not have the necessary training or education. Perhaps they are in a job that is too difficult or one that does not use their specific strengths or talents. Or maybe they have not been given the resources, equipment, staff, funds, or authority to do the job well.

2. They are unwilling to do the job. They have the training, staff, money, and resources. They know how to do the job, but they come to work day after day and choose not to do the job the way it should be done. They have allowed their attitude, negative feelings, apathy, resentment, stubbornness, or just plain laziness to affect their efforts to do the job well.

Employees who are unable to do the job need help. If they have the desire, willingness, and enthusiasm to do what is necessary, they should be given the training or resources they need to contribute successfully to the financial growth of their company. Employees who know what needs to be done, yet are persistently unwilling to do the job, should be history. Poor work performance is no longer an option.

Pay for performance is definitely the wave of the future. This does not mean that companies are not responsible for competitive compensation and satisfactory benefits, nor does it mean that employees should be denied paid vacations, sick leave, maternity leave, or a rare personal day. It does mean, however, that employees should be ultimately responsible for getting their job done even when they cannot be there. And when they are there, they should be 100 percent committed to doing the best job possible. If they are, they should expect raises, promotions, and bonuses. If they are not, their jobs could be in jeopardy.

In the 1980s a story was in circulation that went like this: "By the year 2000, people will be enjoying a four-day workweek—thanks to the computer." And for a while it did seem as if the computer was making our jobs a lot easier. Then all of a sudden the computer broke into full stride, jobs were eliminated, and those that remained required more expertise, more training and education—and more work. Workloads increased as the ability to produce more in a shorter amount of time became commonplace. By the mid-1990s, we were not working just four days a week. We were working longer hours than ever before.

Companies today expect employees to work harder, faster, smarter, and better, according to one of the CEOs we interviewed:

My company needs to get the job done in less time and with fewer people. The other companies in our community are doing just what we are: trying to hire and keep those employees who are willing and able to do that. We all have to work harder and faster. But we also have to learn to work smarter and better.

If that sounds like bad news, the good news is that when you learn how to work smarter and harder, then faster and better usually follow right behind. If they do not, your job could be in jeopardy. Many people find that when they focus on working harder or faster, the quality of their work sometimes slips. Stress is also a common problem. But there are ways to improve your productivity with less stress.

UTILIZE TECHNOLOGY TO YOUR ADVANTAGE

We are all aware of the importance of the computer in today's world. If computers are an integral part of your job, then you already know that they can and do help us work smarter, faster, and better. There are, however, some people who know that computers are important and they have begun to learn how to work with them, but they are not going at it "full steam." If you are one of them, don't wait any longer. Take the time to learn now, because when your company does incorporate computers into your job in a big way, you may not have much time to learn what you need to know. As computers become a bigger part of the picture, having the necessary skills already in place will give you a definite advantage over those who don't.

Or you might think: "I don't understand computers, but that's okay, because I don't use a computer in my job or anywhere else." That couldn't be more false. All of us, including you, use computers every day. Chad, a line supervisor at a glass manufacturing company, agreed wholeheartedly:

We're computerizing our customer service program and some of our employees are complaining because they're scared of what they don't understand. They say they never use computers and don't want to learn. I'm trying to make them see they're already using them when they pump their own gas, check out at a supermarket, place an order at a fast food restaurant, take a book out of the library, or use their ATM card at the bank. I'm trying to turn their thinking around, and I hope we're finally making progress.

Computers have certainly changed the world in the last few decades, and we've only just begun to see the remarkable accomplishments that will take place because of this technology. Everything and everyone is going on-line. Marketing, advertising, and sales will reach out to the waiting millions of people in Cyberspace. We can go to school, purchase goods, advertise products, research and gather information, pay our bills, and communicate with friends and clients without leaving the keyboard. Computers also make us more accountable, since our work can be checked and double-checked, faxed and e-mailed for others to see. Accuracy is more important than ever before.

Because they contain more information than the human brain can remember at any given moment, computers can help us all work faster and smarter. SuLei, a CPA in a large accounting firm, commented:

Our computer program with its built-in spell-check, dictionary, and grammar-check ensures that our clerical staff sends out professional correspondence at all times. The ability to access a huge database in an instant saves us countless hours looking up the information we need to do the best and most accurate job for our clients.

The CEO of one of the top fast food restaurant chains in the country commented on how computers were helping his employees work smarter, with greater accuracy, and saving money in the process:

In the "good old days" our clerks had to figure out the amount of the order, add the tax, and figure out the change due. Now the computer calculates the tax and indicates how much change is due the customer. It doesn't sound like a big deal, but it adds up to millions of dollars being saved every year by giving the correct change. And our customers feel more confident that they won't accidentally be overcharged or short-changed by an honest, yet very busy, employee.

There is probably no business in the world that won't eventually use computers. Carlos, the manager of a large sporting equipment company, voiced his frustration with employees who refuse to accept the inevitable:

My staff has known for a year that we were bringing in a computer system. We've offered Saturday training sessions and night classes after work—and we even bought them dinner! Last week we put the system in place. Most people are okay with it, but we still have a few employees who never found time to go to the classes. They have no idea how to even turn the computer on. They're slowing everyone else down because they can't do the job required of them, but they don't seem to care.

Some companies will not have the time or the incentive to spend money and effort on computer training for their employees. If you are presently in a position where you do not need to use the computer, be aware that this is not the way it will always be. If you cannot convince your company to train you, then learn to use the computer on your own. Monica, a nurse, saw the handwriting on the wall when more and more tasks in her department were being handled by computers. Her hospital would not pay for the training so she took computer classes at night, on her own time, and paid for them herself. She told us:

I'm not entitled to a job just because I've been here a long time. Some staff members have gotten so complacent they flatly refuse to change, even to save their jobs. It was tough going back to school at my age, but job security was my goal.

What are you doing today that could be done faster and better with the use of technology? For example, how is technology being integrated into your communications? Are you making good use of e-mail, cell phones, pagers, fax machines, and modems? These can all be very effective as long as you incorporate "high-touch" (strong interpersonal skills) with your "high-tech" skills and don't forget the need for individualized communication and personalized service.

Meredith, the owner of a toy company, commented on the reasons why her company is becoming more involved with technology:

> Because of the soaring costs of paper and continued postal rate increases, we are redefining our use of paper by asking how we can do business better and faster with less paper. We're using e-mail to communicate on-line with our customers. Paychecks are filed electronically, and all paper shipping invoices have been eliminated. We need employees who are willing to change their ways of thinking and doing, and who are also willing to upgrade their skills to help us reach our goal of saving money and passing the savings along to our customers.

It has been said that this is the age of the entrepreneur. According to *The Futurist* magazine, electronic networks are enabling people "to create businesses with few fixed costs and little or no real estate or weighty bureaucracy." The timing couldn't be better. With companies looking for ways to outsource work or use contract employees to fill many of their positions, the computer provides an added benefit for people who want to start their own businesses.

Look around your workplace. Are you integrating new technology into your present job? Are you on the lookout for new ways of working faster, smarter, and better? Can you be replaced by a machine, and if so, what are you doing about it? Learn to master technology before it masters you.

USE TIME WISELY

Time management is a familiar phrase, but a misleading one because none of us has the power to manage time. But we can manage our response to time and how we use it to our best advantage. Organizational tools, strategic plans, and priority lists are simply devices to help us manage ourselves, not time. The sooner we realize this, the sooner we'll be able to work smarter and better. Greg, a lending officer at a bank, shared his strategy:

> With only so many hours in the day, I had to determine the best use of my time in making money for the bank. So I prioritized my customer list into groups A, B, and C. If someone is on my C list as "least profitable" I determine if there is another department or person who can meet their banking needs while I concentrate on building strong relationships with group A—the customers who are most profitable to the bank. With the B list, I consider how to provide more services, help them become more profitable customers, and move them up to the A list if possible.

Although Greg realized he couldn't create more hours in his day, he knew he could work more efficiently. If we focus only on not having enough time rather than on how we could better utilize that time, we can sabotage our own efforts to be more productive. As an example, the manager of an insurance office compared two employees, Art and Lyndsay, who work in the same department and have deadlines to meet every Wednesday:

> Art starts complaining on Thursday morning about next week's deadline, but he hasn't learned how to organize the process. All week long, he jumps from one project to another, never completely finishing anything. He leaves everything out in plain sight on his desk so he won't forget about it. With all the clutter, he can't see anything, much less decide what to do with it! By Wednesday afternoon, he's worked himself into a frenzy of disjointed thought and action. He

just barely manages to meet his deadline, and on Thursday morning the process begins all over again.

Art's lack of a plan contrasted sharply with Lyndsay's method of meeting the same deadline:

Organizing her activities daily and keeping track as the week progresses, Lyndsay calls her Wednesday schedule "hourglass time." Prioritizing her tasks to meet her various deadlines, she thinks of item A on her to-do list as the first grain of sand falling through that hourglass. She knows she must work on it first before she moves to something else. The other grains, or priority items, follow in order of their importance. She can speed up the pace as more grains fall through, but she's very focused on what needs to be done first before moving on to something else. She consistently meets her deadline without creating undue stress for herself—or for the rest of us.

The difference in how each of these employees approaches a deadline is obvious. Also notice how apparent their actions were to their manager. How would you describe your plan for meeting deadlines, and how does that affect the other people on your team? Just as important, how does it affect your manager's opinion of you and your ability to get the job done?

If you're working as part of a team that's survived a downsizing, you're probably doing the work of several people and you may feel there's never enough time to get everything done. On some days, you leave the office thinking, "I don't know why I bothered to come in today. I'm further behind now than I was when I got here this morning." Betsy, an employee in the marketing office of a large shopping mall, told us about her experience:

Last week, I went to a seminar on my day off to learn how to manage my time better. What a waste! The instructor was totally out of touch. He suggested: Have someone screen your calls. Complete one task before *permitting* anyone to interrupt you, and ask that person, "Can this wait, or could someone else help you?" Great advice for me . . . two years ago. After surviving the most recent round of layoffs, I answer my own phone now, and my job involves being interrupted many times a day, at other people's discretion—not my own. So I have to figure out ways to save time to make up for all the time other people waste for me.

Even with the best of intentions, some people fall into another big time-wasting trap: procrastination. Comfortable with the fact (or the excuse) of putting things off, many of them claim they can't help it—it's just how they are. Or they claim to procrastinate on purpose because they work best under pressure. Although neither of those statements may be accurate, some procrastinators have had a lifetime of success putting things off, not because they really do work better under pressure with last-minute deadlines, but because others have always been there to pitch in, cover up, pick up the slack, and do what it takes to get the project completed on time. They continue to procrastinate because it works. And how does their procrastination affect productivity in the workplace? An employee in a telemarketing firm spoke of a co-worker:

> Colette is a friendly, upbeat person with an outgoing personality who is terrific on the phone. She's going to graduate school while she's working, and she always leaves her term papers until the very last minute. She says she works well under pressure and deadlines, but she's so stressed out that she makes careless mistakes at work—mistakes we all have to pitch in and correct for her.

In another example, a suburban "social scene" magazine with a small staff suffered because of one employee's tendency to procrastinate. An editor who had worked with him for seven years offered her very candid opinion:

> Wes knows well in advance when his part of our project is due. He says he waits until the last minute because deadlines

"bring out the best" in him. The best? He gets short-tempered, he yells and orders people around, and then gets his feelings hurt when we complain about how he manipulated us again. We're a small outfit, and I can't transfer him to another department. So I'm probably going to have to let him go. I can't sacrifice the morale of the entire team for one person.

Because each of us has a unique, one-of-a-kind personality, we all have different ways of mismanaging our response to time. The manager of a packaging plant described his frustration in dealing with several of his employees:

Megan is results-oriented. Her desire to "get it done now" overrides her concern for "doing it right—the first time." Then she uses valuable company time to correct her errors. On the other hand, Marsha is so laid-back, she thinks she has all the time in the world to complete a project. When she gets down to the wire, we all have to pitch in and help her complete a task that was her job—not ours. And Paul—what a perfectionist! He does something over and over until it meets his standards, and he usually misses his deadline. He won't accept the fact that his work doesn't need to be perfect—it just needs to get done!

The owner of a large sales organization spoke of the time and money she had spent sending over five hundred people through time-management training in the last three years, with disappointing results:

I'm tired of wasting our training budget on people who don't want to change. Procrastinators can go to every time-management class in the world, but they have to want to change. Workaholics can attend seminars on balancing home and career and still avoid developing personal relationships. Lazy people can read every organizational manual and memorize every technique yet continue to fail because they're still looking for a way to work without really working. Those who thrive on being in total control can learn all the right management skills and still remain overwhelmed because they won't let go and delegate to others.

When employees are not willing to change unproductive behavior, a supervisor or manager may have to make a change for them by removing them from that job and letting them go. Today's organizations need employees who can honestly evaluate their own strengths and weaknesses and who are willing to change the traits and habits that are keeping them from getting the job done faster, better, and smarter.

USE POSITIVE ENERGY

Negative thoughts and energy create more work for everyone. First, negativism keeps us from focusing on what needs to be done and how to do it. In addition it saps our creativity, impairs our objectivity, and weakens our excitement and enthusiasm for doing a good job. Our attitude about ourselves and our job plays an important part in our ability to get that job done. Austen, the manager of a metropolitan airport which is facing a major reduction in staff, commented:

> Attitude plays an important role in how we respond to time. When our line workers are angry with the system, bitter about their situation, resistant to change, and unmotivated to work, there will never be enough time on their shift to accomplish what needs to be done. In our industry, a poor attitude is one of the biggest time-busters of all. In order to work smart, our employees need to clear their minds so their energy is going into the job rather than into complaining, arguing, resisting, and worrying about things they can't control.

People who are unhappy with their jobs are often tired, even though many of them are not expending any more energy. In fact, some are actually doing less at work than usual. When we're unhappy we tire more easily, give up sooner, and overlook the many possibilities that might help us get the job done better or faster. We lose our energy and creativity and tend to feel more like a victim than the person in charge of our time. Negative attitudes and feelings have a direct impact upon our energy source. To work smarter we have to have a positive attitude about ourselves and our jobs.

TAKE CARE OF YOURSELF

Everyone today agrees that eating healthy food, getting enough sleep, and exercising will all help build strength, both mentally and physically. Still, we don't always do what we know is best for us. In an age of "hurry up," "do it quickly," "it's got to be now," and "don't be late," it's easy to skip meals, put off exercise, and delay getting to sleep because there's still so much to accomplish. And once our heads hit the pillow, we may spend a lot of valuable rest time worrying about our future—including contemplating the likelihood of our continued employment. To work better we have to set aside the time to take care of ourselves and make the commitment to *honor* that time now for a payoff of better health in the future. But sometimes things get in the way. Maria, a travel agency employee, lamented:

> I tried going to a gym to exercise three days a week, but it just didn't work out, so I bought a treadmill I could use at home. But by the time I pick up the kids at day care, stop at the grocery, get home and get dinner going, help with homework, and put the children to bed, I don't have the energy to get on the treadmill. I barely have the energy to fall into bed myself!

Nathan shared what he calls his "guilty conscience syndrome":

> I grew up with my parents always telling me, "When you finish your homework, you can go out and play . . . when you finish cleaning your room, you can watch TV . . . when you

finish . . . when you finish." They set deadlines to teach me how to be responsible. That was good, up to a point. The problem now is that as an adult I'm never finished with all my projects and tasks. And I feel guilty if I take time off just for me. I can't win!

If you don't make time to take care of yourself, who will? Companies today need employees with quick minds, unique ideas, and the physical energy to put them together. The manager of a physical therapy rehabilitation center said:

When we are healthy and our bodies are working well, we can make clearer decisions, cope more effectively with difficult people and situations, and feel more confident to do what needs to be done. While our employees are dedicated to taking care of others, I am constantly reminding them to make sure they take good care of themselves.

Our physical health seriously affects our ability to do our jobs well. While our mental capabilities will help determine how long we stay employed, our physical well-being will help determine whether we can work to our full potential. Staying healthy should be an important priority for your personal and professional security and success. Creativity, energy, flexibility, confidence, and enthusiasm all come more easily from a well-rested, well-fed, and healthy body.

BE CREATIVE

Companies are crying out for employees who can be creative, see new angles, envision new strategies, and motivate others to do the same. When employees are worried about the possibility of losing their jobs, they often become more structured and less creative. Not wanting to do anything out of the ordinary to call attention to themselves, they sit tight and wait it out. But this is not the time to be run-of-the-mill, lackluster, and ordinary. It's critical to stop saying, "I can't," and focus on doing things that send the message "Yes, I can."

Taylor, a mid-level manager in a technology firm, told this story:

Brady, who's been on this job for less than a year, focuses on what won't work, and what could go wrong with a new project. Hal, who has been with us for seventeen years, focuses on how he would begin if he knew he could accomplish this task. Unlike Brady, Hal moves beyond the impossibilities into the realm of possibilities. We're in a constant state of change and we need employees we can depend on for their ability and ingenuity to develop new approaches to old problems. If Brady can't do that, we won't be able to keep him on the team.

When your company is in the middle of a staff reduction, it will be to your disadvantage if you try to blend in with the crowd. Instead, you need to shine. But don't charge ahead full-throttle without thinking and make a serious mistake—or a fool of yourself. Concentrate instead on creative ways to do your job faster, smarter, and better. The CEO of a mid-size hospital in a very competitive market stressed the importance of creativity:

There are three hospitals in this community, and we are seriously overbuilt. As our patient count continues to drop, we constantly have to come up with creative ideas to market our services. We need employees who can help us cut costs, increase profits, and still continue to provide the best quality care we can.

Companies do not want static. They want dynamic. They do not want tunnel vision. They want imagination and creativity. And they most definitely do not want a laid-back attitude. They want energy. Are you doing the same old job the same old way, or are you helping your company accomplish its goals by using your imagination and creativity to their fullest?

HAVE THE CONFIDENCE TO DELEGATE

Because many lean, downsized companies have fewer people to do the work, quite often there is no one to whom you can delegate, as much as you would like to do so. Nevertheless, it is an option that many people overlook. The owner of a tile and carpet company described one employee who intentionally ignored that option:

> Kyle should be sharing some of his workload with others who could help him do the job better. But he's afraid to let go of some his perceived power. Instead of being a team player, he wants to do it all alone. Unfortunately, he's burning the candle at both ends and becoming more and more unproductive.

Learning to delegate appropriate work to the appropriate person is a necessary skill that will enable you to work smarter, faster, and better. In fact, many people work harder than they should have to because they are uncomfortable or unwilling to use the resources and staff available to help them. By delegating some of our workload to others, we can concentrate on doing what we do more effectively and creatively. Are you confident enough to ask for help? Are you trying to do it all and finding you're too tired to do anything well? If so, be careful. There are lots of people around with the skills and the energy needed to do your job and, perhaps, do it better.

Sometimes employees come to work too exhausted to do their jobs because of situations that have nothing to do with the workplace. Delegating and sharing the workload at home is just as important as delegating at work. Both leave you with more time to do the things you need to do more efficiently and effectively. Many people are involved with church and community activities and charitable organizations, which is, of course, a very good thing. But learning to say no when you're overextended, and asking for help when you need it can keep you from becoming so burned out with your outside activities that you don't have the energy you need to do your job.

Learn to enjoy your leisure time

While it's important to work hard when we're at work, it's just as important to enjoy our leisure time when we're not at work. Except for those people whose work has become their entire life, most of us utilize a portion of our paychecks to provide some of the "little extras" which make our time away from work more enjoyable. And that's as it should be. We need to get away from it all once in a while. But unfortunately, our country is one of the few which does not value leisure time. In fact, it's not uncommon to hear someone brag, "I'm so busy that I haven't taken a vacation in years. I just can't get away." Some people believe they're too important and indispensable to take time off. Stephanie, dean of students at a large university, said:

> We're understaffed and overworked, and I keep saying I'm going to take some of my five weeks of accumulated vacation time and visit my grandchildren. But each year comes and goes and I still haven't made the trip. I just wait until they come to visit me. I finally realized this workload will continue whether I'm here or not, and my grandchildren will be grown before I know it. So I'll keep working hard while I'm here, but now I've got my airline ticket to visit my grandchildren for two weeks this summer. While I love my job, there's a lot more to life than that.

Those who control their jobs, instead of allowing their jobs to control them, recognize that they need to take time to enjoy life, friends, and family. Their jobs provide the income and resources to do just that. A healthy balance between our personal and professional lives can bring us great satisfaction and contribute to our physical and emotional well-being. And that, in turn, can improve our effectiveness on the job.

The owner of a lawn and garden center told us:

> I have a manager who prides himself on never taking time off. But the reason he doesn't is because he's not organized,

does not delegate, and does not work well as a team member. As a result I don't see him as a dedicated employee. I see that he is failing to use his time at work wisely.

The mid-level manager of an advertising agency commented:

I can really tell which of my employees had a relaxing weekend and which ones didn't. Some of them come into the staff meeting on Monday morning already tired. I can't help but wonder what the quality of their work will be by the end of the week. The reason I can focus in on that Monday staff meeting is because I've relaxed over the weekend, taken time to be with my family, gotten my mind off my work, and come back charged up and ready to go. I need employees who know how to use their free time to regroup and reenergize, so they can come back to work on Monday and start all over again.

Are you taking time—making time—for fun and relaxation? Do you spend time on any recreational activities or hobbies? The word "recreation" divided into two parts becomes "re-creation." And that's just what we do when we spend time doing something we enjoy. Recreation helps us charge our batteries, re-create our energy, and continue to give our best at work.

We all know people who spend every waking hour at work. We call them workaholics. In fact, being a workaholic has nothing to do with how many long hours you work, but rather the inability to sustain healthy relationships outside of the workplace and truly enjoy your leisure time. People can work sixty or seventy hours a week in a job they love and still have strong and enjoyable relationships with family and friends. This is because they know how to integrate their personal and professional lives. Unfortunately, there are also people who don't understand the importance of doing that until it's too late.

Aaron, a pediatrician, told this story:

From day one, I never set aside enough time for my wife and children. I was a dedicated physician and I was determined to help build up my clinic and increase my patient load. My wife finally had enough, and she divorced me. It has taken me almost a year to get back on track, with the help of counseling. I see now that I was so busy taking care of other people's children that I sacrificed my relationship with my own kids. I still have a thriving practice, but that's all I have..

Although companies are looking for employees who work hard, they also want people who are able to create balance and harmony between their personal and professional lives. Studies show that people who have strong personal commitments to family and friends are happier, healthier, and live longer—obviously benefiting themselves, their families, and the companies which employ them. An important part of learning to work smarter, harder, faster, and better is to stay healthy in mind and body so we can meet the challenges of today's workplace more efficiently and effectively than ever before.

CHAPTER 6

Communicate Openly and Directly

▣ Which employees would I keep? The ones who can most effectively communicate their needs, preferences, ideas, and feelings to their customers, co-workers, and our company.

It seems the one thing that people are communicating about most these days is the need for better communication. It's definitely important in all areas of our personal and professional lives. And yet many people are unclear about what good communication really is. The rhetoric goes something like this: "If only we could open the lines of communication, our relationships would improve, our customers would be happier, and our company would be successful." So if most people agree that good communication is the answer, then what's the problem? CEOs and managers gave a variety of answers:

▣ It's frustrating when some of my employees hold on to whatever information and knowledge they have as though it were some great secret. Sometimes it becomes such an issue of power and control that it reduces their ability to trust one another and work cooperatively as a team.

◉ I have a couple of employees whose look and tone tell me something different than their words. They're angry, frustrated, and annoyed. But when I ask what's wrong, they respond, "Oh, nothing." How do I get to the truth if they won't be honest with me?

◉ Why can't people say what they mean and mean what they say? I share an idea at a meeting and then ask if there are any questions or discussion, and no one says a word. After we've agreed to move on that idea, I hear later that half the group is against it. Why didn't they say something? Don't they understand how important their feedback is to the success of our project?

Employees shared just as many frustrations with the concept of "open communication":

◉ We need top-level management to be honest with us instead of making us work on bits and pieces of information, most of which filters down through the grapevine. They keep telling us to "envision the big picture" but they never let us have a glimpse of what it's supposed to look like.

◉ We literally have to lie to our customers about prices, quality, and shipping dates because we aren't given the information we need. How can we establish a good customer relationship based on exaggerations and untruths?

◉ I'm tired of hearing bad news through terse, impersonal memos and e-mail where I have no opportunity to ask questions or discuss issues.

If a lack of good communication can have a negative impact on how well we do our jobs, it follows that good communication will help us improve our job performance and better our chances for remaining employed. But just what are the components of good communication and how can we communicate more effectively?

COMMUNICATING IN A CLIMATE OF TRUST

What has trust got to do with good communication? Everything. You cannot communicate openly and honestly in a climate of suspicion and distrust. Ask yourself these questions about your company:

- Do employees and management trust each other?
- Are customers getting what they're promised?
- Are managers and employees empowered to tell each other what's really going on?
- Can employees share concerns and feelings without fear of recrimination?
- Is everyone on the team committed to the mission and vision of the company?

Effective communication, the kind that allows relationships and companies to thrive, requires that the participants trust one another, believe in one another, respect one another, and listen to one another. It also requires the willingness and commitment to put ego and hidden agendas aside in order to establish a relationship based on shared values and common goals. It's true there will be times when you have to communicate with people you don't trust—perhaps people you don't even like. You may have to tolerate difficult customers, co-workers, or employers. But don't think for a moment that your relationship with them will include open communication. You cannot substitute tolerance for trust.

Effective and open communication cannot exist without trust. It is necessary because truly open communication is based on a commitment to say and do what is honest, fair, and right—without fear of reprisal. One employee told us:

Our company keeps talking about open communication, but I'm not sure how open I really want to be. I'm so used to not saying how I feel that it's scary to suddenly be asked to share my problems and concerns. I'd like to think it would work. But perhaps I'll wait and see what happens when some of my more assertive co-workers speak out.

RayAnne, a manager for a large appliance store, commented on the climate of trust in her company:

A while back, it seemed we had reached the point where everyone was pretty open. If someone had a problem or complaint, he or she would try to talk to the person face-to-face and work it out. Our managers worked hard to communicate exactly what they expected. In the last couple of years, however, we seem to have regressed. Now everyone acts as if they're scared to say what they mean.

The truth is, sometimes it is scary today to say what we mean, particularly when we feel the need to be careful not to offend people or fear that our words will be misinterpreted or misunderstood. Many managers admitted that their companies often gave mixed signals when it came to encouraging employees to be truly open communicators. According to one human resource director:

On one hand, we encourage employees to take risks, and communicate openly. On the other hand, we don't want them to say anything that might be misconstrued. And above all else, we remind employees to "document, document, document everything you say and do." That makes it difficult to say how we feel. No wonder everyone is clamming up, since that approach appears safer than opening up.

But if you believe you will stay out of trouble by keeping quiet, you may be mistaken. Most CEOs and managers told us they were frustrated by employees who did not communicate. Listen to what the chief financial officer of a major hospital had to say:

Jason has ceased to be an effective employee. He's so afraid of saying the wrong thing and making someone angry. If he can't communicate to other employees the information they need to do their job, or to our customers about our commitment to service and excellence, then he is no longer of value to us. Being sensitive to the feelings of others is certainly important today, but Jason seems to be overdoing it.

Like many other employees, Jason has the mistaken notion that being "politically correct" means giving up honest communication for fear of offending someone. Of course, we should try to avoid giving offense, but that does not mean that we should stop saying the right thing, even though the right thing—the truth—may be hard to say and even more difficult to hear. Padi Selwyn, president of Selwyn Associates of Santa Rosa, California, commented on the consequences of not saying the right thing:

By the age of three, most of us know the difference between the truth and a lie. By the age of ten, most of us have been convinced that telling the truth is usually less trouble in the long run. By the age of eighteen, most emotionally healthy people tell the truth most of the time. Yet by the time we've established our careers, we've learned to be very careful about telling the truth. This doesn't mean we intentionally lie, but we do learn to be diplomatic, politically correct, and sometimes "dishonest" by not speaking the truth, at great cost to ourselves and our customers and clients. Delaying difficult conversations and stinging truths is to delay positive outcomes and opportunities. It's a far greater risk to know and not speak out than to risk the consequences of silent conspiracies and unspoken truths.

A climate of trust in the workplace is crucial because the relationship between employee and employer is an important one, and working for and with people who truly seek open communication based on honesty and trust should be everyone's goal if the company is to succeed. Without trust and mutual respect, a company can talk about "open communication" in every mission statement, slogan, and strategic plan with no visible results. Trust is the foundation upon which open communication is built.

FACE-TO-FACE COMMUNICATION

Talking directly to others is probably what most of us think of when we hear the word "communication." It is impossible for open communication to exist without a commitment from both sides to communicate directly with each other. A climate of trust cannot be developed and maintained in a workplace where gossip, tattling, threats, intimidation, and other forms of manipulation and behind-the-back game-playing are allowed. The problem seems to be that many people do not know how to effectively communicate their concerns, ideas, and feelings face-to-face in a way that will meet their needs, while keeping the relationship strong and healthy.

There are four styles of face-to-face communication: assertive, passive, aggressive, and passive-aggressive. These four styles, each in their own way, affect our ability to communicate openly with others. But assertive communication is the only one of the four that allows us to experience what we like to call "open and trusting" communication. The other three all involve some degree of manipulation, avoidance, or form of game-playing which make it difficult to maintain a relationship built on trust.

Every time we communicate with another person, we can choose one of these four styles in which to frame our thoughts. Open communication can only take place between people who acknowledge that they are responsible for how they communicate. Even though we have become accustomed to using one of these styles more often than the others, we have used all four styles at some point in our lives.

The assertive style is the most effective means of communication, and many visionary companies are offering courses and workshops designed to help their employees communicate more assertively. Although assertive communication is often confused with the aggressive style of communicating, they are actually exact opposites. Assertiveness relies on honesty, openness, forthrightness, and the commitment not to be a victim or play "the blame game." When you are communicating with a person who is using the assertive style, there is a strong sense that you are being told the truth in a fair and tactful way.

The human resource director of a large insurance company described an assertive employee:

> Claire uses "I" messages which are clear and to the point. She states what she needs without attacking, threatening, bullying, intimidating, or making others feel guilty. She's a good listener and she respects her team members' right to voice an opinion, even if it's different from hers. Claire maintains good eye contact and communicates positive messages through her words and her body language.

The manager of a large dry-cleaning chain also shared an example of one of his best employees, who uses assertive techniques with his customers and co-workers:

> Dena cares about people and his professional relationships are based on mutual trust. He is willing to stand up for himself and express his true feelings in an honest, caring way. Even though he is willing to help others, he does not allow others to take advantage of him. He's been at several of our stores in this region in his twenty-two years with the company, and he has earned everyone's respect because people know they can count on him to say what he means and mean what he says.

Aggressive communicators may also say what they mean and mean what they say but they hold nothing back, usually at the expense of others' feelings. The manager of a television station described an aggressive cameraman:

> Pete has a chip on his shoulder, and he acts like he's better and smarter than anyone else. He loves to argue and he usu-

ally wins, but only because people get fed up with trying to reason with him. Others at the station think he's rude, abrasive, and sarcastic. Some have even refused to work with him on different projects. Pete believes others respect him because of his "power," but they really see him as obnoxious and arrogant. They tolerate him, but he has no friends here at the station. It's sad, really, and he doesn't even see what's happening. But he is creating too much tension. We've got to let him go.

People using the aggressive style of communication have one specific goal: to get their needs met by dominating and controlling others. Anger is their most frequent weapon, and they use it to manipulate and hurt others. The supervisor of a medical lab said this about a technician who had gone too far:

There is hardly anyone who knows his job as well as Mark does. But this is the third time in four years he's been on probation and this time, we'll probably let him go. It's too bad, because we'll miss his knowledge and expertise, but no one will miss him personally. His temper is out of control; he will literally say and do anything to get his way. We have employees who are afraid of him—afraid to ask him a question or afraid to point out a mistake or error. We can't promote a team concept with Mark ready to blow up at any moment.

Whiners and complainers can be just as manipulative and hurtful as screamers and intimidators. Naomi, director of human resources in a large computer software company, described such an employee:

Jenny is the world's best martyr. She is always complaining about how much work she has to do—as though the rest of the employees aren't working just as hard. She constantly goes on and on about how hard her life is, how tired she is, and how no one understands her or her terrible situation. The rest of us have problems as well. But Jenny tries to make everyone feel guilty and somebody always offers to help do part of her work plus theirs. It's apparent to all of her co-workers that she is not pulling her weight. They are looking to me to do something. Unless she begins to get her act together, she will have to go. It's just not fair to the rest of the staff.

Why do some people predominantly use the aggressive style? That's easy—because it's so successful. When faced with an aggressive communicator, most people give in, give out, or give up. Aggressive communicators are frequently rewarded for their negative and controlling behavior: better schedules, fewer project assignments, longer breaks and lunch times. What they fail to realize is that a relationship based on guilt, fear, and control can never be successful or healthy in the long term. Aggressive communicators may meet their short-term needs and goals, but they will not create or strengthen the kind of relationships that can accommodate open communication. Although many of us have used the aggressive communication style at various times in our lives to get our needs met, understanding our own tendencies to manipulate and replacing those tactics with assertive techniques is the secret to becoming a better communicator.

Unlike aggressive communicators, people who communicate in the passive style seldom say what's really on their mind. Their main objective is to avoid a confrontation at all costs. They often put their needs last in an attempt to be liked by everyone and to please those around them. It's sometimes wise to walk away from a confrontation if it's not worth the hassle. But if the passive style is used too often, people can get into trouble. In their attempt to please everyone, they usually end up pleasing no one. André's manager told this story:

André has a hard time denying someone's demands or requests, even if they're unreasonable. Since he doesn't like to make anyone angry or hurt anyone's feelings, he has a difficult time saying no. That's commendable at times, but André doesn't realize he has a tendency to let others take advantage of him. He is always agreeing to take on new projects and ends up not following through or turning in rushed, inaccurate work. It would be better if he were honest with others about what he can and cannot accomplish successfully.

Because the word "no" is not usually in the passive communicator's vocabulary, they often go through life feeling victimized and put upon. Gloria, a staff member in a large nonprofit association, is an example:

Because we're a nonprofit entity, we operate on a shoestring budget. Consequently, we often don't have enough people to do the work. People are always dumping projects on me that no one else wants. I've already got all the work I can handle, but I don't complain. I don't want my co-workers to think I'm being uncooperative, so I just smile, grit my teeth, and say "Sure, I'll help you out." I guess I've just kept my feelings hidden inside for too long. Lately, however, I'm always depressed and I've started having bad headaches. I don't even want to go to work anymore.

Unfortunately, feelings can only be hidden inside for so long. An advertising executive told us this story about one of her employees:

Joel doesn't realize it, but he's like a time bomb. He doesn't express his anger in a positive way. It builds up until he explodes over a trivial incident and vents his anger on the unfortunate person who happens to be around at the time. Then he feels guilty and apologizes, but pretty soon, we know another blowup is inevitable. He doesn't complain when clients take advantage of him; he just smiles and takes it. But his wife has told me that he brings that anger home and takes it out on her and the kids. Although I've suggested it several times, he's not willing to go for counseling. If he refuses to change, I can't afford to keep him on staff.

It is difficult to count on passive communicators. Helen, district manager for a retail clothing company, told us this story about one of her salesmen:

> Cliff loves people and is very enthusiastic about his job and his product. We were so excited when we hired him. Now we have found there is another side. He doesn't want anyone to be angry or upset—ever. So he lies. He lies to customers about delivery dates that he knows we cannot meet. He lies to me about his number of sales so I won't think he hasn't done his job well. Doesn't he realize that we all find out the truth sooner or later? Then we really are angry because he wasn't up front with us from the beginning. We're going to have to let him go, because we simply can't believe what he says. It's a real shame. He's such a nice guy!

Companies cannot depend on employees who communicate passively. They seem so accommodating at first. The difficulty comes later when the passive communicator is asked to be a contributing member of the team and doesn't want to share honest feelings and opinions. Open and honest communication is built on trust, and passive communicators fail to say what they really mean.

The passive-aggressive communication style is probably the most difficult one to deal with in a relationship. Passive-aggressive communicators avoid confronting others and steer clear of face-to-face discussions (passive) but they nevertheless want to get their own way or make others suffer (aggressive). And they usually do it behind another person's back. They may gossip in the lunchroom or tattle to the manager. This style of communication is laced with deceit and secretiveness because it is always done undercover. It is usually hurtful and can even be dangerous to a company. A surprised CEO said this about one of his department managers:

> Carla is the last person I would have suspected to be working against me. She always seemed so supportive, both in

meetings and in one-on-one conversations. When I asked her opinion, she always indicated that she agreed with my ideas and plans. Then I found out she was the one getting the rest of the employees upset and angry—telling them my ideas would never work and that I had never consulted her. I'm angry, but I'm also hurt and disappointed. I don't understand why she did this.

Unfortunately, most companies have a couple of firmly entrenched passive-aggressive employees like Carla—and a few apprentices waiting to take their place when they retire! It's easy to understand why companies would like to identify these "snipers" and move them elsewhere. Passive-aggressive communication is the exact antithesis of the open and honest communication necessary for a company to thrive.

Good, solid businesses that believe in outstanding customer service and quality products need employees who have the ability to communicate assertively. But most of us communicate without any thought or planning. And because we have never been taught about these four communication styles, we are often content to say whatever comes into our minds. We usually react rather than think about how we will communicate. Remember, all of us have a choice about which communication style we will use in each and every situation.

Look around your workplace and try to notice how people communicate. What style do you choose most often? In many cases, assertiveness is chosen far less often than its more negative counterparts. Most of us weren't raised to ask questions, negotiate, and debate issues. Assertiveness takes serious planning. We must think before we speak if we want to communicate assertively.

Are you willing to focus on communicating with others in an assertive way? Can you help create a more trusting environment where employees can enjoy working together? Do you avoid gossip and tattling? Do you let people know what you need instead of waiting for them to read your mind? If so, then you are exactly the kind of communicator good companies want to hire and keep. Today's organizations need people who are excellent communicators, not only with their customers, but with their co-workers as well. Communicating assertively is vital if you want to have a positive impact on your customers, your co-workers, and your organization. Why? Because it sends a message that you are an employee who has the ability to state your needs and wants while at the same time considering the needs and wants of others.

NONVERBAL COMMUNICATION

As you may know, only a very small part of our message is communicated through the words we use. The rest comes from body language, gestures, tone of voice, and facial expressions. A shrug of the shoulders or a nod of the head may tell us what someone is really thinking, although their words say something else. Eva, department manager of a large insurance claims office, described such a case:

> We have one employee who rarely speaks, but her facial expression and body language say it all. In the two years she's been working here, I've never seen her smile. The minute she comes into the office, it's like a dark cloud descends over us all. It's as though she wears a big neon sign that says, "Don't bother me!" And it works. We all avoid her, but it's not fair. We're doing her work as well as ours.

Misunderstandings can run rampant when people send mixed messages. Here are some of the most familiar ones in the workplace:

- ▣ *"Oh sure, I would love to help you."* (through clenched teeth)

- ▣ *"No, I don't have a problem with that."* (eyes rolling)

- ▣ *"Sure. Fine. I'll be happy to work on that project."* (while heaving a deep sigh)

- ◙ *"Of course I'm not angry. Why should I be angry?"* (loud voice and exaggerated gestures)

- ◙ *"Yes, sir, I'll be glad to give you a refund."* (snatching receipt from customer's hand)

Have you gotten mixed messages from your co-workers like these? Were they confusing? And how did they affect your ability to trust the person who sent the message? Tune in to your own nonverbal communication and consider times when you may have sent a mixed message without realizing it.

Mixed messages also come in the form of well-meaning phrases that create doubt in our minds about what people are really saying. They're usually spoken out of habit, and are sometimes used as introductory phrases. But they certainly can confuse the listener who is trying to decipher what you really mean. Here are a few common examples (with a typical response in parentheses):

- ◙ *"To be perfectly honest with you . . ."* ("As opposed to being dishonest, which you usually are.")

- ◙ *"I shouldn't be telling you this but . . ."* ("So why are you telling me?")

- ◙ *"The fact of the matter is . . ."* ("Here comes one of your off-the-wall opinions.")

- ◙ *"Now, I don't want to get anyone in trouble, but . . ."* ("If you don't want to get someone in trouble, you wouldn't be tattling.")

- ◙ *"This is going to hurt me a lot more than it's going to hurt you . . ."* ("I doubt it.")

Many employees underestimate the importance of nonverbal communication. Ben, the district manager for a national bookstore chain, told us this story:

I know we're going through a lot of change and it hasn't been easy. But two employees are really making it difficult. Oh, they never say anything—at least not to my face. But you should see them at meetings. No matter what I say, they roll their eyes and give each other an impatient look. It's so obvious. When I ask them what's wrong, they always answer, "Nothing, boss." Well, I know better and I just don't trust those guys.

To build and maintain a climate of trust, mixed messages, whether verbal or nonverbal, cannot be part of the picture if you want to communicate openly and honestly with your co-workers and your customers. Try to develop insight into your communication style, identifying your strengths and targeting areas for improvement. In addition to the words you use, eye contact, body language, facial expression, and tone of voice are all very important. But you must also include the many parameters of voice quality, intonation, intensity, and energy, all of which are a part of a person's "vocal image." Often, it's difficult to determine if your vocal image needs help. Ask someone you trust—a friend, family member, or colleague—to give you some honest feedback. It can be a valuable learning experience. That's what Patrick, a sales manager, did:

I was scheduled to do a major presentation for an important client and I asked one of my salesmen to critique me with the use of a home video camera. Was I surprised! I squinted, grimaced, and even rubbed my nose a few times. Although I was very passionate about our product, I certainly did not convey that passion during "rehearsal." In fact, there was no excitement in my voice at all. I almost put myself to sleep. Needless to say, I made sure to get some coaching from a professional who helped me correct my bad habits and improve my speaking skills. It was one of the smartest things I've ever done.

It's important to remember that while family, friends, and colleagues can offer valuable and helpful feedback, they are sometimes so accustomed to our little habits and idiosyncrasies that they become oblivious to our communication faults—just as we do. To them, these faults are "just how we are." Or perhaps they love or admire us so much that they don't notice (or feel uncomfortable discussing) the problem. It is wise, however, to pay close attention when an employer, manager, or supervisor does notice—particularly when they observe that some aspect of our communication style is below standard. Joan, a management consultant, explained how feedback from her manager had probably saved her job:

> I had been with the company for only a year. During my performance appraisal, my manager said that although I was very knowledgeable, several of my clients had complained that I was difficult to understand because I spoke so softly, which made me appear unassertive and unsure of myself. They were uncomfortable working with me because they were not totally convinced I knew what I was talking about. On my manager's advice, I got a professional evaluation from a speech coach. This has made a real difference in my interaction with clients and co-workers because now I sound confident and assertive. The time I invested with my speech coach was invaluable. My clients have much more confidence in my abilities and my "new and improved" communication style has helped advance my career.

Take an honest look at your communication style, both the words you use, and they way you deliver them. If you think you may have some areas that could stand improvement, don't waste any time getting the help you need. An effective communication style can help you attain success in any career.

LISTENING SKILLS

The other important part of effective communication has nothing to do with talking; it has to do with listening. Most people would agree wholeheartedly that good listening skills, or the lack of them, send a powerful message to other people about how much the listener respects them and their opinions. A branch manager had a very negative reaction to the poor listening skills of one of his employees:

Three minutes after Tyler has been introduced to a potential customer, he can't remember his name. He tells me it's because he's busy thinking about what he's going to say next, and what kinds of services he can begin talking about to get him to move his account over to us. When that customer comes into the branch the next week, Tyler invariably calls him by the incorrect name. It doesn't seem to bother Tyler, and he just laughs it off. But the customer isn't laughing, and it certainly makes him feel unimportant. Tyler had better improve his listening skills or be prepared to move on.

A CEO had this to say about one of his sales reps:

When Kirk and I are discussing his failure to meet his sales projections for the quarter, I can tell he is not listening to my ideas and suggestions. He's too busy preparing his defense, arguing, rationalizing, and making excuses for why he didn't meet his quota. If he would talk less and listen more, he could get his sales back up to where they're supposed to be. I'm just about ready to give his territory to Sascha, one of our top sales reps. Sascha listens to my suggestions and then acts on the feedback I give him. He's moving up rapidly in our company, and his strong listening skills will help him get where he wants to go.

Although many of us recognize the importance of being good talkers and work to develop that skill, we may not spend enough time developing our skills to be equally good listeners. Why is listening so important on your job? One CEO explained it this way:

I don't sit around staring into space and creating the "vision" of where we need to go. There is a lot I don't know, and the only way I can learn is to listen to people who do know. I don't always have to follow their advice, but I do need to listen.

An employee compared the listening abilities of two of her colleagues:

Talking to Trina is a good use of my time, because I know she's listening to me. She asks questions, makes comments, and most important to me, she looks me in the eye when I'm talking to her. Dave, on the other hand, is always looking everywhere but my direction. He makes me feel unimportant, like he would rather be somewhere else, talking to anybody else but me. I've simply stopped sharing my thoughts and ideas with him.

A manager talked about what a great listener his CEO is:

Grant really makes communication a priority in our department. He takes time to listen when I have an idea. If he thinks my idea is a good one, he gives me the confidence to write it up as a proposal or implement it on the team. If he doesn't believe the idea is workable, he asks questions that help me discover that for myself. I always learn a lot about myself when I talk to Grant.

Contrast that example with the following comments from an employee who felt his manager did not know how to listen:

Christen has an open door policy. She says to drop in any-time we have any questions, concerns, or suggestions. When I do stop by her office, however, she makes me feel as if she's much too busy to talk with me. I ask if I should come back later and she says, "No, go ahead, I'm listening." Then she continues to clear off her desk, review her phone messages, sign papers, and do anything else that needs doing. Later, she never remembers what we've talked about. No wonder! She wasn't listening! Talking to her is a complete waste of time.

Most people won't say what they honestly think and feel unless they believe someone is listening and attempting to understand what they are trying to say. A human resource director described such a situation that existed between two departments in her company:

> Their unwillingness to work together had reached the CEO's ears, so he brought them all together and I facilitated the session. After some time we learned that a disagreement four years earlier had fostered the present feud, and since that time, no one had listened to anyone else. There was no communication and, consequently, no trust. Through guided facilitation, they began to work toward building a climate of trust and mutual respect. Although it took several months, both departments finally learned to really *listen* to the needs of the other people involved, and when they began listening, they opened the door to cooperating with each other.

How about you? Are you working to develop and maintain a climate of trust and open communication in your workplace? Listening is an important part of that goal. In order for a trusting relationship to develop, both sides must believe their needs, ideas, and feelings are understood. That does not mean they always have to agree. But agreements are much easier to reach when there is mutual understanding.

Electronic communication

While we know communicating electronically can save us time and money, it's important to remember that how we use that technology can help or hurt our efforts to communicate effectively with our customers and our colleagues.

Voice Mail

Your voice mail message creates an impression with the person at the other end of the line. Here are some widespread complaints:

- ▣ I was looking for an outside consultant about motivating my employees. And when I reached his voice mail, it was the most uninspired, low-energy message I had ever heard. How could this person motivate my employees if he couldn't even motivate himself to leave a more positive and professional message?

- ▣ My pet peeve is when I call someone and I have to listen to them sing or tell a joke before I can leave a message. If it's a long-distance call, I get pretty ticked off. If I wanted to hear a song or a joke, I would turn on the radio. This, to me, is very unprofessional. I won't call back.

- ▣ I called a firm whose outgoing message was very professional, but before I could leave my message, I had to listen to seventeen beeps that registered how many other messages they had. Maybe I was supposed to be impressed with how busy they were, but I was too busy to hang around until it was finally my turn. I hung up and called their competitor, and we're doing business together now.

A purchasing manager expressed the most common complaint:

Call waiting on a business line is rude. Recently, while talking to one of our suppliers, he put me on hold in the middle of our conversation. He was gone for quite a while, and then he came back on the line and told me he would have to call me back because he had to take this other call. That sent me a message. I may let it happen once, but not twice. Instead, I'll find people who make me feel like they really want to do business with our company.

Effective communicators avoid those mistakes. They use their voice mail messages to "put their best foot forward"—even on the telephone:

- When I'm leaving a voice mail message, I try not to make it sound so rushed that people think I'm in such a hurry I won't call them back anyway.

- I always stand up when recording my voice mail message because it gives me more vocal energy. I put a smile, along with enthusiasm, in my voice.

- I pay attention to what I'm saying. I write down or script out the important facts—even the entire message—before I record it so I don't sound disorganized, repeat myself, or leave out important information the caller needs to know.

- I don't waste callers' time singing to them or sharing my favorite joke or my positive thought for the day. Their time is money, and I think they will appreciate my being brief, concise, and professional.

- I don't have call waiting. If I'm on the phone, another caller can leave a message on my voice mail and I'll return the call as soon as possible.

Your voice mail creates an instant impression for the caller who has never met you in person. Make sure that it's a good impression.

E-mail

As with any form of electronic communication, e-mail has its benefits. However, it, too, can get out of control. One CEO complained:

Many people have gotten into the habit of sending long-winded e-mail messages instead of trying to get in touch with me personally. By the end of the day, I can print out a roll of paper long enough to wrap around my office. I don't have time to read all that stuff. If you really want to get through to me, call me on the phone.

A manager described her frustration with e-mail:

I'm going crazy. People who would never send me a letter through the mail have put me on their e-mail copy list. People I really don't consider to be my close friends are sharing their thoughts, problems, events, situations, predictions, illnesses, deaths, and even their holiday messages with me. Leave me alone already!

Perhaps a good rule of thumb would be: if you wouldn't write people a letter or call them on the phone with this information, then resist the temptation to e-mail them. This medium is not the place for frustrated writers, poets, advertisers, and therapists to get their untold secrets, problems, and advice out to the entire world.

Another employee voiced this concern:

Our supervisor is trying to keep us all in the information loop, but too many of us don't need to know everything he wants to share. I've received messages where he copied fifty to a hundred people. Rarely do a hundred people on our team need to hear the same message unless it's a change in policy or a short announcement. I wish my supervisor would quit making me waste my time reading all his e-mail messages and let me do what I'm getting paid to do—my job!

E-mail can also become a never-ending accumulation of messages with each person afraid to stop this techno-conversation for fear of hurting the other person's feelings or not having the last word. We need to create a mannerly, congenial way to end a conversation that has gone on far too long. One manager told us about trying to end an e-mail exchange with a manager from another facility. It went like this:

<OK-I think we've come upon a great solution. Let's try it out
and get back later to check our results.>
<Great. Let's do it. I'll be back in touch soon.>
<Fine. I'll wait to hear from you.>
<OK-I'll touch base in a couple of weeks when I get back from
vacation.>
<Good-I'll be out, too.>

And on and on it went, time and energy (and money) wasted saying absolutely nothing. Remember, how you use e-mail can say as much about you as your voice mail messages. If you want to create a good impression, keep your e-mail brief and to the point.

WRITTEN COMMUNICATION

In our verbal communication we have the opportunity to correct misconceptions, make ourselves more clearly understood, and even repair potential damage we may have caused through an incomplete or inappropriate expression of our thoughts and ideas. By becoming aware of and modifying our nonverbal signals, we also often have a second chance to correct someone's opinion of us and our ideas. Written communication, however, is not as forgiving. The written word doesn't give us many second chances to get something right or to correct misconceptions we may have created. The image we create of ourselves and our ideas on paper is a lasting one. The marketing director of a large radio station expressed her amazement at the lack of professionalism of a firm she was considering:

I just received a letter from people at an advertising agency in response to my inquiry about using their services for one of our new community awareness campaigns. As soon as I began reading, two misspelled words practically jumped off the page at me. Of course, they're off my list as potential suppliers. Why would I give my advertising business to a company that is not 100 percent accurate in their own daily correspondence? Why would I think they would proofread my brochures and press releases any better than their own correspondence?

Your ability to communicate in writing—through reports, letters, memos, proposals, and other means—may be very important to the overall success of your department and your company—and to your employability. While most people recognize the importance of good writing skills, some admit to having a harder time than others. One employee commented:

> My wife is fantastic at spelling and grammar and has wonderful written language skills. Me? I can't even get my kids to play Scrabble with me. They say I invent words that don't even exist. Seriously, I'm a terrible speller, and my written work reflects it. If it weren't for spell-check on my computer, I'd be up the creek.

This man is a good example of someone who recognizes his weakness in a part of his communication and has taken advantage of the tools he needs to help him improve. But not everyone does, as evidenced by this comment from a frustrated manager:

> Mark insists that his poor writing skills don't matter. He has the tools to help him, like a computer software program that checks spelling and grammar. But he won't take the time to use them. He represents our company every time he corresponds with a customer. If he's not willing to improve his skills, we can't keep him on staff.

No matter where we work and what we do, our customers, like most of us, are usually overwhelmed by too much information and not enough time to read all of it. Although our written communication is one way to strengthen our ties with our good customers and create new bonds with potential customers, some employees don't think it really matters. The owner of an office furniture store complained:

Trisha is spontaneous in her conversation, and it's one of her greatest strengths with our customers. But in her written communication, that spontaneity is causing problems. She never takes time to edit or proofread her correspondence, and she thinks people will overlook her mistakes because they know how busy she is. They're busy, too, and they are not impressed with her lack of accuracy.

Committing to the time and energy to improve our writing skills often leads to unexpected payoffs and rewards. Lewellyn, an employee in the customer service department at a bank, shared this success story:

I was always asking my peers to proofread my work and correct my errors. But they began to resent my taking their time to help with something I should know how to do—and they were right. So I signed up for a seminar to polish my writing skills and worked hard at putting my new skills to work as fast as I could. And guess what! I got really good at it, and now some of my peers are coming to me and asking for my help. My supervisor has noticed, too, and she has given me some additional writing assignments which will help me move up in our department.

Effective communication is more important now than ever before. Because communication is what business relationships are all about, companies need employees who can communicate openly, honestly, and assertively. Those who can do that will add immeasurably to their value and increase their potential for long-term employability.

CHAPTER 7

Look for Leadership Opportunities

◉ Which employees would I keep? The ones who are willing and able to assume a leadership role and take charge when necessary and appropriate.

You may not consider yourself a leader in the traditional sense, but when we use the term "leader" we are not referring only to those who hold a titled leadership position, such as supervisor, manager, human resource director, employer, or CEO. We're talking about everyone in the organization because all employees must be able and willing to assume a leadership role when the need arises, regardless of their job title. In fact, many companies have eliminated titles like foreman, supervisor, and department manager to reinforce the belief that each employee is a contributing member of the team with leadership potential, depending upon the task at hand.

If you don't see yourself as having leadership qualities, then you'll miss many opportunities to demonstrate your added value to your employer, co-workers, and customers. Being a leader simply means you are willing to teach and support others, be a positive role model, and be ready to serve as well as lead. Effective leaders can be found at every level in an organization. Even if you work under someone else's leadership, you can still be a leader in your ideas and attitudes about your job.

The office manager of a law firm described how one of his employees demonstrated leadership skills:

Denise, our receptionist, reports to three different attorneys. Even though she's only been here two months, she's already demonstrated her leadership abilities. One day recently, all attorneys were out of the office when an important document was delivered by courier and we had to respond by five o'clock. There was no one to talk to or check with about how it should be handled, but Denise called the right people and followed all the correct procedures. In these circumstances, I can't tell you how important it was for Denise—who normally would not have been responsible for these duties—to be willing to accept a leadership role. Without her, we might have lost an important client.

The manager of a grocery store recounted a similar story:

One day when I was out of the store, a salesman came in and we had to place an order immediately to take advantage of a substantial savings on a particular item. Ralph, our head cashier, knew this was a product we wanted to keep on our shelves and he also knew we were running low. He saved us a lot of money by being willing to make the decision to place the order without waiting for me. Ralph showed the initiative and decision-making ability of a true leader. He's now been promoted and does most of our ordering and fulfillment.

Both Denise and Ralph were confident when it came to taking the lead because their companies had empowered them to make decisions, demonstrate leadership abilities, and solve problems. However, we've all had experiences with employees who do not feel empowered by their organization even when it comes to serving customers.

Jean's son Michael had a particularly frustrating experience. After he paid a sizable deposit to have the electricity turned on in his new apartment, he waited all day on Friday (as instructed by the customer service rep) for a technician. When no one had arrived by late afternoon, he called the utility company and was told by an operator that because someone had lost the paperwork, it would be Monday before the electricity could be turned on. This was more than a minor inconvenience, since the low temperature predicted for that evening was 17 degrees! Michael objected, but it was as if the operator was on automatic pilot. All she could do was repeat, over and over: "I'm sorry, sir. Our policy is that we can't fill orders after four o'clock and our technicians don't work on the weekends. You'll just have to wait until Monday." It didn't seem to register with her that her customer had paid to have the service turned on, and the lost paperwork was not his fault—or hers. Each time she said, "There's nothing I can do," Michael replied, "That's not an acceptable answer. I would like to speak to your supervisor."

Finally (very exasperated with this *bothersome* customer), the operator put him through to her supervisor, who apologized for his inconvenience and said someone would come immediately (even if it was after four o'clock) to turn on the electricity. The phone operator was not empowered to make a decision to help a customer. And with such restrictions placed upon her by her company, would she ever see herself as a leader with decision-making ability? Probably not. In an age when customer service is top priority, conditions like that could cause some companies to lose valuable customers.

Whatever business you're in, there are probably other companies that provide a similar service or product. Today's consumers have many choices, and they usually choose to do business with the company that gives them the best quality and service. One manager told us:

> Our reputation for good service depends on our employees' ability to make decisions and do what is right for our company and our customer. To survive and thrive in today's competitive world, we need employees who are focused on

service, who can see the big picture, and who are not afraid to take charge when the need arises.

Although companies say they need employees who are willing to assume a leadership role when necessary, the term certainly has a very different meaning today than it used to. In times past, we referred to our leader as "the boss." The people at the top of the organization "bossed" their employees by telling them what to do and when to do it. If employees asked a question or came up with an alternate (or better) idea, they faced the real threat of being told they were insubordinate or, even worse, being fired for "rocking the boat" just once too often.

Then CEOs and managers began to notice that when employees were "bossed"—when they had no sense of importance or ownership in their department or their company—most of them tended to do only what was required and nothing more. Eventually, leadership began to take a different turn. Terms such as "quality circles," "site-based management," and "empowerment" came on the scene. Companies began to value the ideas and insights of the employees who were closer to the customer, the products, and the services they provided. One CEO admitted, with some embarrassment:

> It took us long enough, but we finally saw the importance of having employees at all levels, not just in top management, who could recognize leadership opportunities and demonstrate their confidence and ability to follow through and make tough decisions. Encouraging this behavior has definitely helped us become a stronger company.

Even though management agreed on the need for strong company-wide leadership, it was difficult for them to agree on a definition for leadership that applies to all employees in all situations. The dictionary definition of leadership is "a guiding force," "an influence," "the ability to assert authority over others." In his book *Leadership Is an Art*, Max De Pree, chairman of Herman Miller, Inc., takes it a step further: "Try to think about a leader, in the words of the gospel writer Luke, as 'one who serves.' The art of leadership is liberating people to do what is required of them in the most effective and humane way possible. Leaders are also responsible for future leadership. They need to identify, develop, and nurture future leaders."

De Pree's definition of leadership is a far cry from the usual definition of the word boss. The bosses of the past seldom thought of themselves as liberators, would have been insulted to be referred to as anyone's servant, and wasted little time and effort nurturing their employees.

Whereas bossing implies tight-reined control, leadership in today's terms implies just the opposite: the ability to let go of control and allow others to do what they were hired and trained to do. In a country where power and control often go hand in hand, the whole concept of letting go and delegating has been difficult for many managers and CEOs. However, as members of top management become more and more proficient in their new leadership roles and learn to be facilitators, coaches, and teachers rather than dictators, enforcers, and supervisors, they soon realize how important it is to have employees with strong leadership qualities at every level of their organization—not just at the top.

Paradoxically, many managers expressed their reluctance to delegate even as they encourage others to try out their leadership skills. The head pharmacist of a large national drugstore chain confessed:

Fifteen years ago our store was small and I was the only pharmacist here. Because I am a perfectionist, I would usually double-check every prescription to make sure it was correct. Now our store is five times as big and I have four people working under me. I struggled to let go of control, but I still rechecked everything my employees did. I finally saw them as highly skilled professionals who could be trusted, so I had to back off and let them do their jobs. I now train, teach, oversee, and coach, but I no longer stand behind them and look over their shoulders. I must say that being a leader is far more challenging and exciting than being a boss.

If every employee is expected to assume a leadership role when the need arises, then it becomes imperative for each of us to know what abilities we should have in order to be perceived by those around us as effective leaders. We've all heard the term "born leader." While it may be true that some people seem to fall into the role of a leader more easily than others, it is possible for most of us to develop the abilities that will help us take charge, motivate others, and make good decisions. The CEOs, human resource directors, managers, and employers we interviewed listed the qualities they believe describe a good leader. Let's take a look at each of them and see how they apply to the organizations of today.

LEADERS ARE TRUSTWORTHY AND ACT WITH INTEGRITY

In today's business environment where teamwork is crucial, there can be no doubt that all employees must be able to trust and be trusted by their co-workers. Good leaders don't criticize their co-workers behind their backs, and they don't take credit that belongs to everyone on the team. Instead, they build trust by openly admitting their mistakes rather than blaming others. They give credit where credit is due, and they help others celebrate their successes.

The owner of a large photo finishing process distribution center described one of her most valued employees:

> As a district manager, Hunter has worked hard to create an environment of trust and honesty with every team of employees in each one of our stores. Our employees know they can always count on Hunter to keep his word. He's good at expressing what he needs from each employee and he takes co-workers' feelings and ideas into consideration as well. I can always depend on him to do what's right, even though it might not be the easiest, or the most expedient, thing for him to do.

Leaders build trust with customers and co-workers by acting with integrity. They make sure their words and actions are congruent all the time, not just when it's convenient. Another manager told us:

> There is nothing more important to me than being able to trust and believe in my employees. I don't have the time to watch over them and check up on them. I expect honesty on every front, from their sick leave to their expense account.

Many employees think it's acceptable to call in sick when they aren't, or "beef up" their expense accounts "because everybody else does it, and the company doesn't know or doesn't care anyway." Everyone we spoke to agreed wholeheartedly that when employees behave like that, not only do their managers notice, but their co-workers notice as well. Needless to say, employees who cheat their employer do not stay employed for long.

LEADERS ARE HIGH ACHIEVERS WHO STRIVE FOR EXCELLENCE

In the book *The Super Achievers,* the National Institute of Business Management defines an achiever as the person "who consistently performs at a high level of effectiveness." In other words, an achiever gets the job done and does it well. The institute identified two strong characteristics of high achievers:

> An extraordinary amount of physical energy; and
> A highly competitive spirit.

Bill Marriott, chairman of the Marriott corporation, is a good example of a high achiever. He logs more than two hundred thousand miles a year visiting the various properties his company owns. When asked why he travels so much, he responded: "If you're going to be a star performer, you can't sit back and relax. A star performer has to work hard and make sacrifices, and at Marriott corporation, we do both."

Do you see yourself as a hard worker—as a star performer?

Even though you may not own the company, do you own a sense of pride in your work and your ability to contribute? How strong an achiever are you? Do you see yourself as striving to outperform others and set new standards of excellence for your department and your organization? A good leader must have a strong desire to be the best by providing outstanding customer service and working hard to create an excellent, cohesive, and productive workforce. Do leaders always succeed at the task? No. But the important thing is that they keep working at it.

The manager of a large apartment complex told us about Heather, who showed her leadership ability by going above and beyond her customers' expectations:

> Heather leases more apartments than anyone else we know. She remembers every potential tenant and writes the most wonderful thank-you notes, commenting on things they had told her while looking at an apartment, such as an upcoming wedding or new baby. She does everything she can to help ensure their move will go smoothly, and she has a small welcome gift waiting for them when they arrive. No wonder everyone wants to rent from her. They feel like they've made a new friend!

Many employers who talked about their employees' leadership abilities mentioned words like "perseverance" and "determination." Leaders keep working to be the best they can be. They stay focused on their goals, but they keep things in perspective and realize that there is always room for improvement. They continually strive to learn more about themselves and their jobs. They integrate excellence into every task.

LEADERS MAKE OTHERS FEEL IMPORTANT AND VALUED

Leaders value other people's worth and opinions and take the time to let them know they are important. It doesn't take very much time to pay someone a compliment. The average is six seconds or less. "I like your suit. Is it new?" "Thanks for giving me a ride to work. I appreciate it." "Great report. Keep up the good work."

Criticisms, complaints, and negative comments, when they are necessary, should also be kept "short and sweet." The average complaint too often goes on and on, and the person being criticized feels angry, resentful, or humiliated rather than challenged and motivated to do it right the next time. Leaders, however, know the power of the compliment and constructive criticism. They take the time to pay compliments and keep their negative feedback brief and to the point. That way they make others feel important and valued, while offering concrete suggestions on how to improve.

We can also make both our co-workers and customers feel important by asking questions, listening, and tuning in to their needs. For our co-workers questions such as "Do you need some help?" "Do you want me to listen for your phone while you take your break?" demonstrate our ability to tune in to their needs as well as our own. Imagine how important our customers feel when we ask questions such as "How can we get better at delivering the service you deserve?" "What are our strengths?" "How can we improve?"

Have you, as someone's customer, ever been asked to share your thoughts and ideas about how to improve service? Maybe it was through a telephone survey, a questionnaire enclosed in your monthly billing statement, a suggestion box in the lobby, or a face-to-face encounter with someone in the organization who felt your opinion was valuable. Wouldn't you be inclined to continue doing business with a company that made you feel important and let you know it valued you and your business?

Contrast those feelings of worth as someone's customer with an experience I (Jean) had while trying to explain to the manager of a shoe store why I was returning a particular pair of shoes. The woman interrupted me in mid-sentence, snatched the receipt from my hand, and said, "Look, lady, you'll get your money back. I'm really not interested in hearing your life story." Was this employee exhibiting good leadership by making her customer feel important? And what do you think the chances are that I will give that store any more business?

Smart companies know that employees who feel valued and important will treat their customers the same way. One manager told us:

> We understand that our employees must feel valued in order to do their best, so we spend time asking them what we in management can do to help them be more productive. We also ask them about procedures that make their job more difficult, and we're open to making changes in those procedures when we can. We can't always do everything our employees recommend, but we're open enough to ask the questions, listen, and act on the feedback we receive.

The CEO of a small community hospital commented on the value of a patient services representative who makes patients (customers) feel important:

> Sarah treats all our patients with dignity and respect, and people feel comfortable when they are with her. Many of them come from miles away. They have other hospitals closer to their homes, but they come here because they like how they are treated. Sarah is responsible for building that rapport. As a result of her leadership, our hospital is the one that patients choose.

In your leadership role, how generous are you with positive words and actions? Are you committed to helping others feel better about themselves? Do you value people and their ideas? Making others feel important and valuable could help make you invaluable to your company.

LEADERS ARE POSITIVE ROLE MODELS

Values are difficult to teach. We usually learn to be honest, trustworthy, loving, compassionate, and sensitive by observing and interacting with others who have integrated those values into every aspect of their lives. Leaders serve as role models for how people should live their lives, personally and professionally, by making decisions and behaving in ways that consistently reflect high values.

The owner of a cellular telephone franchise talked about the leadership traits he valued in one of his top sales managers:

Troy is a strong role model for the other salespeople on his team. They look to him to see how things should be done, and they see how he treats his customers and co-workers. He's honest, sincere, and unselfish. Troy understands that his attitude and behavior at work reflect our high standards and our commitment to excellence.

Sometimes it's easy to forget that others are observing how we conduct ourselves as we do our jobs. But we are all "on stage" when our colleagues and co-workers look to us to set a positive example. How about you? Are you a positive role model, the kind of person others would emulate and respect? If you were looking for a role model, would you choose someone like yourself?

LEADERS ARE WILLING TO SERVE OTHERS

To some people, serving others may seem like the role of a subordinate, not a leader. But in fact, a good leader believes in service to others. If that sounds contradictory, think of words such as "cooperate," "help," "work collectively," and "share" because they more accurately reflect the true nature of service to others.

The owner of a video store told us of a longtime employee who was skilled at putting her own ego aside and concentrating her efforts on what was best for the team and the company:

When Laura retires next year, it will be difficult for anyone to fill her shoes. In the eight years she's been here, she's been a real leader in her department. She's always ready to pitch in and do whatever needs to be done. I've never heard her say, "That's not my job." I've personally seen her stay past quitting time to help another employee who was struggling with a difficult problem or an unhappy customer. Her commitment to service is outstanding. Even though she's a department manager, she's never felt she was too important to do any job—from changing a lightbulb to filling the vending machine. If it needs to be done, Laura is willing to do it.

Many employees shared their frustration with co-workers who refuse to help others and whine "But that's not my job." Every employee may have a specialty such as accounting, maintenance, or sales, but there is never a guarantee that any of us will always be able to do just what we specialize in 100 percent of the time. Companies need employees who are willing to help each other. As one manager put it: "Maybe if we all pitched in and looked around to see how we could be of help to others, everyone could go home on time once in a while!" The future will demand that people learn new skills outside their areas of expertise and use them to support other team members, even when it's "not their job." Are you willing to do what is needed even if it doesn't fall under your specific job description? Leaders support their co-workers when it counts, not just when it's convenient.

"But what about those of us who would prefer to follow rather than to lead?" you may ask. "Can't we just continue to do our own jobs? What if we don't want to take charge and make decisions? It's too hard, too stressful, and too much work!" That is a valid point, because every organization, every company, every team needs people who can be counted on to willingly do what's asked of them. But the ability to follow is an asset only if you are also confident enough and able to take the leadership role when necessary. If you only feel comfortable in the role of a follower, your future employability could be in jeopardy. Listen to what a manager said about an employee who had great promise, but ultimately never measured up:

> Benita seemed like the perfect employee at first. She was so nice, and was always willing to help and do whatever she was asked. But I soon realized that's all she does: exactly what she is asked—and no more. She does not take the initiative to look around and see what needs to be done. I need employees who can take charge of things when I'm busy, at lunch, or at another store. I need people who are capable of taking a leadership role.

Even when it's time to stand back and let someone else take the lead, it's important that we continue to analyze, process, and implement the duties and goals laid out for us. Following someone blindly is usually nonproductive if we accept no responsibility for the outcome, and therefore feel no sense of ownership in our own future or the future of the company.

LEADERS ARE CONSUMMATE TEACHERS

If you think back to some of the teachers you had during your student years, there are probably a few who stand out in your mind. You may remember them, even years later, because they were not only good teachers but also good leaders. What were the qualities and abilities they brought to the classroom that made them memorable? Were they good listeners who were interested in their students' opinions? Were they eager to share their knowledge and insights with vivid examples and stories instead of just reciting facts, figures, and formulas? Did they have a sense of humor and know that learning could be fun and entertaining? Could they be trusted to keep their word? Did you always feel they wanted you to succeed, and were willing to help you reach your goals? Were they tough, yet fair? Did they help you grow and develop, not just as a student in their classroom but as a person with potential and a belief in yourself and your future?

The teachers you remember probably had most of these capabilities, which are also the same capabilities we look for in good leaders. Good leaders are good teachers, and good teachers cannot help but be good leaders. Therefore, it is important that all of us work to develop our teaching skills. The supervisor in a federal government agency told us about a leader and teacher in his organization:

> Instead of keeping good ideas to himself, Randy is always willing to share them with his team members. He coaches others in a nonthreatening way, even though he has more seniority than anyone else in his department. If he notices that someone else could be doing something easier, faster, or better, he takes the time to offer some help. People appreciate his advice because it's given in a positive, helpful, and friendly manner. They know Randy wants them to succeed, and they value his suggestions as guides to help them be more successful. He is like a great teacher who is always there, waiting to help his employees learn and grow.

Most people would agree that a good employee should be willing to teach, coach, and be a mentor to co-workers. However, others admit that they used to enjoy helping and teaching their colleagues, but over time they had stopped sharing so willingly. Why? "If I teach everyone else what I know, why would my company need to keep me around?" was a common reply. It's true that at a time when companies are asking employees to network, build teams, and share experiences, employees are often afraid to do just that. Knowledge has become power in many situations, and the employee with the most knowledge often feels the most secure. But the majority of the people we interviewed agreed with one CEO who warned that this is really false security:

> We need people who are willing to work as part of a team and share what they know so others may learn. We are very sensitive to employees who keep information and ideas to themselves because they think it will safeguard their jobs.

When it comes down to deciding who stays and who goes, we will keep those who are willing to share their knowledge and experience to help our company succeed.

Effective leaders don't hoard information and ideas because they know that knowledge is only power when it's shared with people who can implement the vision which that knowledge represents.

LEADERS ARE RELATIONSHIP BUILDERS

Teamwork is a popular buzzword in today's workplace. And it looks easy when we watch an exciting sports event and see everyone working together, putting personal glory aside for the good of the entire team. But if you ask those who have ever coached a team, they will tell you how challenging it is to take a group of individuals and teach them to work together, trust one another, and support one another. An effective coach knows how to build good relationships so that individuals care more about the good of the entire team than about themselves and their own personal glory. An effective leader is able to do the same thing with the members of his team.

In the workplace, employers need employees who can "run with the ball" by themselves when necessary, as well as build and maintain good team relationships. What qualities make someone the most valuable player in the eyes of their employer? The owner of a very successful restaurant talked about one of his top managers:

Steve has worked hard to build solid working relationships with our staff. He gets to know them and their families, and he's a great listener. Since most of our waiters are part-time college students, Steve helps them coordinate their schedules during exam time so they can pitch in and cover for each other. His example has carried over to our employees, who volunteer to put in extra hours for a special event or a busy night. They pitch in and don't complain because they think of themselves as a team. And they sure have had a great "coach."

Do you work actively to build good team relationships? Hopefully so, because it is an important part of being an effective leader. Equally important are good relationships with clients and customers. In today's world, many companies do business with people they barely know, sometimes people they've never met. But the most successful and rewarding transactions, more often than not, involve parties who have developed a solid business relationship. Good leaders understand the importance of building good relationships with their colleagues and their customers.

LEADERS COMMUNICATE EFFECTIVELY

Every CEO, manager, human resource director, employer, and employee must be able to state what they need, want, or prefer with confidence and in a manner that is clear, honest, and forthright. But good leaders must go even further. They must be able to interpret the needs, wants, and preferences of their colleagues and customers to create a cooperative and successful work environment. They must also be able to demonstrate respect for others through their words and actions.

One CEO told us that he had to make a difficult decision to terminate a technically competent employee because he didn't have effective communication skills:

Frank was one of the best technicians we ever had. He could come up with statistics and numbers faster than anyone else. Although the information he collected and compiled was needed by other employees so they could do their jobs equally as well, Frank could not seem to communicate his findings to others in a timely and consistent manner. He missed meetings, failed to respond to e-mail, and ignored other employees' frantic pleas for help. He never seemed to realize that his job was only as good as his ability to integrate his knowledge with that of his co-workers for the good of the company. Frank never understood we needed a leader—not a loner.

Effective communication is the cement that binds an organization together. It is the foundation upon which successful teamwork and good customer relationships are built. It is no accident that employees who can communicate effectively and assertively soon find themselves in leadership roles.

LEADERS ARE OPTIMISTIC, ENTHUSIASTIC, AND HAVE A VISION FOR THE FUTURE

Often it is not what we tell our co-workers and customers, but how we tell them that may affect their willingness to buy into our ideas. A supervisor with a metropolitan area cable company commented:

> Pam's enthusiasm for her projects—and for the ideas of the other people in her department—is contagious. She sets the tone for her department because other employees watch her reaction to situations and events, and they follow her lead. Pam understands that if she isn't fired up about projects and events, she can't expect anyone else to be.

Notice that being enthusiastic doesn't mean you have to be loud and obnoxious. Enthusiasm, according to Dale Carnegie, is a feeling that comes from the inside. "The way to acquire enthusiasm is to believe in what you are doing and in yourself and to want to get something definite accomplished. Enthusiasm will follow as night follows day."

Good leaders are proud of what they do and believe strongly in their company and the products and services they offer. They are realistic about the future and excited at the possibilities ahead, both for themselves and their companies. And they very rarely complain about what can't be done. Instead, they focus on what can be accomplished with hard work and determination. They have a positive attitude about themselves, their jobs, and their lives in general. Their enthusiasm is contagious, and colleagues and customers are energized by listening to them. How about you? If you told others, "I really love my job!" would they react with surprise? Or would they respond, "Oh, there's no doubt about that. It's easy to see that you really enjoy what you do."

Leaders use their energy to project their company's vision to everyone around them. They know the work they do today is the foundation for their future and the future of their company. For example, some people who were touring a NASA facility asked one employee who was working on the line, "What is your job? What are you doing?" She answered, "Not much. I just put this piece into another piece and pass it to the next person." As they continued down the assembly line, they asked the same question of another employee. Her face brightened with a smile as she answered, "I'm helping to build the next space shuttle." Now there was an employee with vision. She sees the big picture and is proud of her role in it. Unfortunately, some employees get so caught up in the routines of their jobs that they forget the real purpose and importance of what they do.

How would you answer the question: "What is your job?" Your future may depend upon your ability to answer this question with the big picture in mind. Good leaders can see far beyond the moment, and they continually strive to put tomorrow on today's agenda.

A GOOD LEADER IS RESILIENT

While striving to incorporate all of these nine leadership traits into their lives, good leaders also realize that everyone slips up now and then. They don't try to be perfect because they know that everyone makes mistakes. But no matter what happens, they don't give up. Instead, they bounce back from setbacks and try again. They understand that no one can do everything without some help, and that no one can be all things to all people. Sometimes they may be having "a bad day" and their "vision for the future" is a little cloudy. Good leaders aren't daunted by looking at this list of traits and saying: "Oh, I could never do all that." Instead, they may say, "Okay, there are some worthwhile goals to strive for. Let's see what I want to work on first."

While leadership may come naturally for some, for others developing strong leadership skills takes thought, practice, and hard work. We believe it's definitely worth the effort, because these skills will benefit all of your personal and professional relationships. Leadership skills are life skills. Being a good leader is a twenty-four-hour-a-day job. If these are skills you've been neglecting, start developing them now. Today's companies need employees who are ready and willing to lead at a moment's notice. Your leadership skills and abilities will help determine your present and future employability.

CHAPTER 8

Commit to Lifelong Learning

▣ Which employees would I keep? The ones who are constantly learning and willing to help take the company into the future by keeping their knowledge and skills up-to-date.

In today's business climate, no one's job is completely secure. Your job may be necessary today but that does not mean it will be necessary tomorrow. The company you work for now won't look the same or be the same in the next few years. Remember, the world is changing quickly and each change has the potential to affect your company and your job. We can never again take our jobs for granted. It is imperative that each of us understand and anticipate future trends that could ultimately change the nature of our job—or even render it obsolete. Let's look at the banking industry. Several years ago, a bank teller told us:

I thought my job was as secure as you could get. How in the world could a customer make a deposit, withdraw money, or transfer money from one account into another without dealing with an employee like me? But things are different now. My bank is encouraging customers to complete all their banking transactions at ATMs through paper transfers. We're even charging our customers fees for using a teller to help with their transaction instead of using the ATM or banking by mail. I saw my job was in jeopardy because an ATM machine doesn't need paid vacation, sick leave, maternity benefits, or a retirement plan. I've gone back to school at night, and I'm earning my accounting degree next semester. I've put in for a transfer to the accounting department. I need to stay employed.

You should never forget that your job will remain vital only as long as it provides the resources, information, and services necessary to your company's success. A regional vice president in charge of several large car dealerships told us:

If my managers choose to ignore the handwriting on the wall, their jobs will be in jeopardy. Our industry is undergoing major changes in the way we sell cars. Some people have even predicted that the car salesman will soon be a thing of the past. Car shoppers can now log onto the Internet to look over the options and compare prices. There are auto brokers available who can negotiate for the customer and do the wheeling and dealing most consumers hate to do. Customers can comparison-shop at auto malls and used-car superstores. Our employees must understand what effect the future will have on our industry and begin to integrate these changes immediately in order to be prepared for what's ahead.

Jobs within almost any business you can name are being totally revamped in order for companies to remain competitive. Are you aware of the trends that might bring about serious change in your company in a year? In five years? How will these trends affect your job? What is your future going to look like? If you want to stay employed, you must know what will be expected of you down the road. What skills do you have that will be obsolete? What skills will be needed that you do not yet have?

The CEO of a hospital commented on the changes in the health care profession:

Health care reform is upon us. I'm not talking about a political agenda for health care reform, but a humanistic agenda. There is no doubt that our industry needs to reduce costs. And one way to do that is to find ways to keep people healthy. Many of our hospitals are already branching out into their communities to teach people what they need to know to stay out of the hospital.

Health care employees will continue to have jobs in the future but they will probably have different jobs. Many employees who once dealt with illness will now have a job that focuses instead on wellness. People who once worked within a hospital will now be going into homes, schools, and companies. How are health care employees preparing for this major change? The human resource director of a large metropolitan outpatient clinic explained:

Some of our employees are taking steps right now to reeducate and train themselves for future changes because they understand how their jobs will be affected. Others are doing nothing to prepare for the future, except to complain about how unfair this system is. Eventually we will reach a point when we have to reduce staff, and I'll keep those employees who have incorporated the future into their plans.

The field of education is also experiencing major changes. Educators are realizing they must do more than teach a predetermined curriculum from kindergarten through college. Instead, they must educate people to become lifelong learners, capable of assessing and assimilating new information throughout the remainder of their lives. A school superintendent remarked:

I've witnessed vast change in my thirty-five years in education. The advent of the computer into our lives has made computation and memorization skills less important. Now we are insisting that teachers supplement and enhance their basic curriculum with skills that teach critical thinking, mediation, and problem-solving. We are beginning to focus on learning rather than on teaching to help our students become productive members of society, effective employees, concerned citizens, and cooperative adults. Our students must leave school well-educated, but also motivated to continue learning throughout their lives.

Computer technology has dramatically altered what we are taught—and what we are able to teach ourselves. What does this mean to the field of education? The phrase "customer service" is a new concept for many educators because they are used to a captive audience. Unfortunately, some educators do not view students as customers they must work hard to retain in order to keep the business of education alive. But that perception is changing quickly as more and more charter schools and private schools offer students alternatives to public education.

Business and industry will look different in the future, too. Computer technology is changing the way we manufacture, advertise, sell, promote, negotiate, collaborate, research, train, and educate. It is also changing the way we do our jobs—and with whom. To find out if you are prepared for some of these changes, ask yourself the following questions:

1. Are you prepared to work many different jobs, each at a different location?
2. Would you consider the possibility of working from your home? Employees in every business are now doing that, especially parents who want to stay home with their children.
3. Are you willing to work more days with fewer hours, or fewer days with more hours? Both are possibilities.
4. Who will be your co-workers in the future? Analysts predict that by the year 2000, the workforce will be 62 percent women, 16.5 percent African-American, and 14 percent Hispanic.
5. Do you have the skills necessary to serve customers with different cultural backgrounds, concerns, and communication styles? Today the trend is toward doing business with customers all over the world.

All the knowledge we have today about technology will represent only 1 percent of the knowledge that will be available in 2050. In other words, we can never stop learning. There will always be more to know. And the more you know, the better chance you have of staying employed. How have you responded to technological changes, as well as all of the other changes that are going on in the workplace? Do you accept new responsibilities and challenges and see them as opportunities to increase your value to your employer?

IDENTIFY THE SKILLS THAT ARE OF VALUE TO YOUR COMPANY

To assess your value to your company, you must be aware of the skills you possess that help make you a valuable employee. Analyzing your skills objectively is the place to start. First, determine what you are good at doing and then take an honest look at how many other employees in your department or your company possess the same, or similar, skills. Some companies place a high value on specialists who are very good at one thing, while others value more generalized knowledge across a wider spectrum. To remain employable, it's important that you know where your company places greater emphasis. If you are not aware of your strengths and their value to your company, it is probable that you aren't using them to their greatest advantage. Even if you are aware of your strengths, start expanding your level of expertise and learn new skills to increase your value.

Although effective self-evaluation must be an ongoing process, it is also important that you have an honest, regular assessment from your manager or supervisor. More and more companies are going a step further to implement what is termed a "360 degree evaluation" in which each employee receives feedback from supervisors, co-workers, colleagues, subordinates, and customers. Remember, in health care the patient is the customer and in education the student is the customer. All customers have the right, and should be encouraged, to provide meaningful feedback that can improve the product or service they use. According to one human resource director:

> This is definitely the most valuable assessment, because it allows employees to see how they are perceived from every angle, and how they can work to improve each and every relationship that is important to their job.

In evaluation, perception is the name of the game. You can have all the right motives, justify your behavior, and defend your attitude to the hilt. But if your boss, co-workers, colleagues, and customers perceive you as apathetic, irritable, argumentative, or impatient, then that is their reality. And you need to address it, not by tirelessly defending your actions, but by working to understand what it is you say and do that creates this perception in other people's minds. It takes great confidence, even courage, to ask for honest feedback. What you basically need to know is:

1. Do you think my job and what I bring to my job are necessary and vital to this company?
2. Why or why not?
3. What can I do that might have an even greater positive impact upon our customers and on the growth and success of our company?

For most of us, the truth is not always easy to hear, but it is usually beneficial if it leads to self-improvement. As one employee put it:

> Every couple of months, I work up my courage, take a deep breath, and ask my manager to tell me how I could run my department better. He shoots from the hip and doesn't mince words, but I really need to know how I am perceived, even if the feedback is negative. That way I can learn to grow and get better at proving my value to the company. For me, that makes more sense than waiting until that feedback is attached to my pink slip.

Managers throughout the country often express their desire to learn how to fairly evaluate their employees and then effectively communicate that assessment. They want their evaluation to validate their employees' strengths yet motivate them to improve their skills. Effective leaders know the importance of honest evaluation and are eager to incorporate that process into the daily relationship between employer and employee. As one manager told us:

> I have worked hard to evaluate my employees fairly and accurately. I realize there should be no surprises on a performance appraisal or annual review. My employees know, day to day, what I expect and how I feel about the job they do. There are no hidden agendas. I want them to be the best they can be, and only through honest evaluation will they be able to meet that goal.

KEEP YOUR SKILLS UP TO DATE

Even if your skills are of current value to your company, you must be prepared for the future. The vast majority of people who lost their jobs due to downsizing or cutbacks told us they knew of the possibility that their jobs might be eliminated—even months in advance. Nevertheless, they did not go back to school, network, or train for another job in their own company, or look into the possibilities of other employment or of starting their own business. Most did not even have an updated résumé when they received the bad news. What about you? Are you preparing for the possibility that your job may be eliminated in the future?

What new skills and training will you need to keep your current job? Often employees mistakenly believe that whatever training they need will be provided by their company. That's not always the case. Although many progressive companies implement fine training and education programs, there are just as many that do not. Marcia, a receptionist, told us:

My first day of work was last Tuesday. I thought the first week or so I would be trained and work with an experienced employee until I learned the job. No way! I was shown a desk, a filing cabinet, the phone, and a manual, and given a ten-minute lecture on how to do my job when my first customer walked in the door. I was left totally alone to handle the situation. I can't tell you how many mistakes I made.

In many companies, this kind of on-the-job training is the rule rather than the exception. Marcia kept her job, but only because she volunteered to come in early for the first few days to spend time with the person who was on the shift before hers. It would be far better if every company realized the importance of adequate training. But if your company doesn't, don't make it an excuse to stop learning. You are in charge of how much you know. A young advertising assistant told us:

I swore when I graduated from college that I would never set foot in a classroom again. But as I looked around our firm, I saw that the people at the top of my profession were those who never stopped learning. They were always talking about the latest class, seminar, or workshop they had attended. When I heard we may be downsizing within the year, I decided to go back to school. I still don't know if my job is in danger, but with the marketing skills I've learned, I've picked up some part-time jobs on the side that will keep me going if I get laid off and I need to look for a new full-time job.

A retailing executive commented on how important it is for his employees to continue developing their skills in various areas:

Our company recommends classes in people skills and problem-solving—anything that will help our employees bring more value to the job. We're willing to pay for the classes, but they have to take the initiative to sign up. We don't push them, but we do notice which employees are developing and enhancing their skills on their own time, and which ones are content to just coast along.

What new skills do you need to acquire, and which of your present skills need enhancement? Perhaps you could develop your computer skills, enroll in a class or attend a seminar, learn better people skills, become a better problem-solver, or improve your writing skills. The list of possibilities is endless. Most of you, however, are working longer hours than ever before and the thought of going to school at night or taking a class on the weekend may be something you don't want to think about. But the thought of being unemployed might be even more staggering. An education and training director offered this advice:

> Be thorough in your research so you have a clear idea of what new skills you must acquire to increase your worth and value in your company. You must have skills which will set you apart from others who are competing for a similar job, and you must have the skills necessary to possibly compete for a new job in the future.

Once you determine the skills you need, then arrange to get that training in a way that is the least disruptive to your life. First, check with your company. A plant manager who approved training at his site made this comment:

> Remember to approach your company with a well-formed plan based on the premise that this training will "directly or indirectly contribute to better customer service and the financial growth of the company." Without this link, your request may not be approved.

An employee who has a full-time job, plus family responsibilities, took an alternative route:

> My company didn't offer any training, so I took some computer classes that were offered near my home. I didn't want

to add another two hours to my already busy day or be away from my kids, but I could see the handwriting on the wall. I told my husband I had to do this and I needed his help. He agreed. I completed the courses just in time. When layoffs came around, they eliminated almost all the employees who had no computer training. I kept my job. Was it worth the six weeks of hassle and $300? You bet!

And finally, this very creative idea from a meeting planner:

Several of us wanted to learn how to use the Internet more effectively to communicate with one another, as well as with destination management companies and hotels. So we hired our own personal tutor, a computer consultant who worked with us on Saturday mornings, and we split the cost. A couple of our co-workers declined because they were angry that our company wouldn't offer the training free on work time. Well, I think they're sorry now. The few hours and dollars we spent made our jobs so much easier. I wish my company had been able to see how this training would help us provide better service to our customers, but I'm not going to risk my job because of it.

There is a wide variety of options to meet your training and educational needs. An additional benefit is the opportunity to meet and learn from other people if you will only step outside your comfort zone to get to know them at training sessions and workshops. It seems amazing in today's rapidly changing job market that there are still employees who feel (and show) that they have no need to learn anything new. This is not the time to demonstrate a lack of interest in learning anything new—not when a commitment to learning is so necessary in order to stay employed.

FIND A MENTOR AND LEARN FROM A PRO

A mentor is a wise and trusted teacher or guide who can help to ensure your future employability. Having a mentor is another way to sharpen your skills and acquire new ones. You may have thought that someone you admire is far too busy to have time for you. In fact, many people are willing to share their knowledge and experience with those who want to learn. But several employees told us they would never ask for help or advice. Don, a division manager, said:

> Ask another division manager for help? You've got be kidding! I've been here longer than any of them. What could they say to me that I haven't already thought about and done? Besides, letting other managers know you have problems or questions tells them you don't know what you're doing. With all the cutbacks, I need everyone to believe I'm doing just fine with nobody's help.

Don doesn't get it. Although all the other managers met regularly, discussed ideas, supported one another, and worked as a team, he refused to participate. Instead of being viewed by upper management as a "guy who had it all together" (as he thought), he was seen as "a guy who will not work cooperatively with his teammates." Don's job is in trouble—and he doesn't even know it.

How do you find and work successfully with a mentor? One mid-level manager told us about his experience:

> I identified a key professional in my industry and wrote him a note, briefly explaining that I would like to meet with him to ask some specific questions about how I could advance my career. I let him know I was willing to meet at his convenience, since he is so busy. When we met for lunch two weeks later, I brought a prepared list of questions to save time. I took brief notes and then filled in the details while the meeting was still fresh in my mind. I followed up with a thank-you note, and he has agreed to meet with me again in

three months to see what I've accomplished from his suggestions and to continue our process. His advice was invaluable, and it helped me set a new course for myself to move forward in my company.

As you can see, this "mentee" was organized and considerate of his mentor's busy schedule, as well as appreciative of receiving some very helpful advice. Contrast that with this executive's experience:

I took time from a busy conference schedule to meet with someone for lunch. Since we only had an hour, I asked him to bring a list of specific questions. Sure enough, he came with only one question: "Since you're the marketing expert, would you tell me everything I need to know about marketing?" Besides the fact that it would take three days to tell him everything he wanted to know, I noticed he wasn't prepared to take any notes. When I commented, he said, "Oh, I don't need to write anything down. I'll probably remember most of what you tell me, and if I forget anything, I'll just call you and you can refresh my memory."

Another top achiever mentioned this call she got from someone in her business, asking for her advice:

We talked for forty minutes, and when my phone bill came I realized that the person had called on my toll-free number. Not only had I given freely of my time and expertise, but I ended up paying for the call without knowing it. It's not the cost of the call that bothers me. But such a lack of consideration and just plain bad manners will make me think twice about being taken advantage of again.

Many employees find mentors in their own companies who contribute to the success of their careers. Remember that most people are willing to help as long as they feel that it's a good investment of their time and knowledge. No matter what field you're in and how much you know, there are people who can teach you something more. Make sure you take advantage of any opportunities you have to learn from the pros in your business or profession. It is an important part of your commitment to lifelong learning.

It is also important to keep reading anything and everything that will enhance your value to your company and advance your career. Do you subscribe to professional magazines and journals that relate to your business? Do you keep up with other reading that does not relate directly to your job but will help your overall employability? Professional journals will often give you more up-to-date information about your business than you can get from people within your own company.

In addition to reading, we encourage you to network, ask questions, and attend in-service training programs to determine how you fit into the big picture. If you don't see your job as a part of that big picture—as part of the future of your business and your company—what can you do to change that? Make sure you join business associations and attend conferences. They provide the opportunity to meet your "competition" firsthand, see what the latest trends are, and make new friends.

You may think you don't have time to implement all of these ideas. But if you want to stay employed, you have to *make* the time for lifelong learning. It's the only way to ensure lifelong employment.

CHAPTER 9

Keep Your Options Open

You, and you alone, are responsible for taking charge of your professional life. And you owe it to yourself to keep your options open. That does not mean that you begin to think about your future on the day you find yourself out of a job. It means that you must think about other opportunities and directions you may take while you are still employed.

Many employees we interviewed admitted they knew they should be looking at other opportunities but they felt disloyal doing so. Some also said they felt guilty for having a résumé, for networking, and for keeping an eye open for other options while they were still being paid by their company. Loyalty in today's workplace is quite different than it was in the past. If your company cannot guarantee you a job (and in most cases it can't), then your future may depend on keeping your other options open and exploring new opportunities. Think about it: your company's executives are certainly keeping their options open. If they can merge with another company or if they have an opportunity to increase profits by downsizing, they will do so. Their ultimate loyalty is to their stockholders and their customers.

Employer and employee both, however, have a responsibility to avoid taking advantage of one another. Fair treatment and compensation in return for a good day's work are still part of the mutual loyalty bargain. When he headed Apple Computer, John Sculley shared his philosophy:

> You're asked to pour a part of yourself into the success of the company. In many ways the individual is asked for a greater commitment than in the days when he or she was simply a cog in the wheel of a systematized organization. In return, you should get an experience that sharpens your instincts, teaches you the newest lessons, shows you how to become self-engaged in your work, gives you new ways of looking at the world. . . . I'm not asking for open-ended loyalty. I am asking for people who are at Apple to buy into the vision of the company while they are here.

Note Sculley's phrase "while they are here." It defines loyalty in today's ever-changing workplace. In other words, while a company is keeping you on the payroll, loyalty is important. But guarantees and promises can no longer be given from decade to decade or even from year to year. In these times, loyalty is a day-to-day commitment.

Often employees talk of their desire to "get all this downsizing and restructuring over so we can go back to work." They say they will then feel safe again, secure in the knowledge that they escaped their worst-case scenario—being laid off. But reengineering and restructuring are ongoing processes. Massive cutbacks may not always continue to be a part of that process because companies will eventually reach a level of employment below which they cannot go and still properly serve their customers. But the *kind* of employees a company needs will change, depending on its goals at any given time.

Let's suppose that you work for a hospital. Anticipating future trends, the decision-makers in your hospital have chosen three major objectives to help them meet their number one goal of making a profit. They want to:

1. Continue to be the foremost provider of health care in their region;

2. Increase their home health care nursing staff; and
3. Build a new rehabilitation wing staffed with professionals who can provide patient care and market this new service to the community.

Your hospital's executives then determine what type of employees they need to accomplish these goals. At this point, they have four hundred employees and believe they will still need four hundred on staff. But to have a staff that meets their new objectives, they will have to lay off some employees, many of whom are doing a fine job but whose knowledge and talent do not meet the criteria necessary to accomplish the new objectives. To fill those slots, they will then begin to hire people with the credentials and experience in the home health care and rehab fields—employees whose jobs are directly linked to the hospital's new goals. A new team has now been formed.

When these three objectives have been met (maybe a year later—maybe five years later), new objectives will be formulated. Once again the hospital executives will decide what kind of employees they need to accomplish their new objectives. They will compare the skills of these employees with their current staff and once again realign their workforce to form a new team qualified to move in an entirely new direction. This process will be an ongoing one. New teams will be formed and re-formed over and over as the community grows and technology changes. This same restructuring process is occurring in every industry—including yours.

If you are serious about staying employed, you must be willing to move from one team focused on a set of specific objectives to another team focused on a different set of objectives, perhaps in a different department, or even within a different company. Or you may consider becoming part of a new group of "permanent temporaries" who work for companies that need employees to fill specific slots for a limited amount of time (weeks, months, or years) to work toward specific objectives. Many of these employees actually like their new roles and see some definite advantages.

▣ I didn't think I would like working as a "clerical temp" but it has really been a good option for me. In addition to picking and choosing where I want to work, I'm getting on-the-job experience in a wide variety of work environments. And when a company is looking to hire a full-time person, I think I will have an advantage over other applicants because I've shown them what I can do on the job.

▣ I've been working as a temporary for over eight months. I wouldn't want to do this forever, but it has taken some of the pressure off. I'm making enough to pay my bills, and I have more time to look for a better full-time job, instead of having to take the first thing that comes along, even if it's not what I really want.

Outsourcing and the use of contract employees are becoming increasingly popular because they enable companies to hire workers in a very cost-efficient way, without the additional burden of providing expensive compensation and benefit packages. In the future companies will have fewer managers, each working with teams of ever-changing employees. Where do you fit in this picture? Where will you fit in the future? What options do you have? Remember, the eight high-performance abilities that we have been writing about will not guarantee that you will keep your job. But they will guarantee that you have the best possible chance of staying employed. Let's look at how these eight high-performance abilities can also help you plan for your future and keep your options open.

1. TAKE CHARGE OF YOUR PERSONAL LIFE

The quality of your personal relationships is always important, but especially during those times when your job is in jeopardy—or even nonexistent. Many employees who have been hit the hardest by downsizing are men and women who have worked tirelessly to move upward in their companies, often at the expense of building and maintaining strong personal relationships. They have literally immersed themselves in their work to the point that their jobs become who they are. They are often shocked when they lose their jobs, and if they have allowed their personal relationships to falter or even fail, they may find themselves without anything or anyone to give their lives meaning.

Being out of work is usually painful for anyone, but the situation can be manageable and even tolerable with the support of friends and family. Those relationships, however, must be built and nurtured along the way. They don't magically appear on demand when we need them. When people lose their jobs, the question is: have they sustained other relationships which will help them experience the transition more easily? If not, the feelings of isolation can be somewhat overwhelming.

Brian, an insurance specialist, told us this story:

I did nothing but work for thirty years. When my wife would ask me to spend more time with her and our two daughters, I'd always answer in an irritated tone: "Why do you think I'm doing all of this? It's for you and the kids." But I knew deep down that wasn't true. They never demanded the big house and the fancy cars; those were for me. I *needed* to succeed for reasons I'm not even sure of. Now my job has been eliminated. My wife and I barely speak, and my daughters stopped asking to spend time with me long ago. I'm left to wonder what it all was for, and I feel very alone. The sad thing is, it's no one's fault but my own.

Jack, a placement counselor for a personnel agency, told a very different story:

After thirty-six years with my company, I walked in one day and was told I had a month to wrap up my projects or turn them over to another department. My job was being eliminated. That was six months ago. After a few weeks of self-pity, I took stock—with the help of my wife. We decided to look at this as an opportunity to do some things we've never done. We sold our big house and bought a smaller condo in Florida—a place we'd always wanted to live. My wife had been a travel agent and I was good at marketing, so we started a small agency. My income is a third of what it was, but my wife and I love our new life. I can't believe I'm saying this, but losing my job was not the worst thing that could have happened.

In the last few years there has been quite a change in the balance between home and work. Many top-level executives have voluntarily chosen to step down or find another job with less responsibility because they were no longer willing to sacrifice their personal freedom, relationships, leisure time, and even their emotional and physical health. Developing and maintaining strong personal relationships takes effort, but it is often these very relationships which will continue long after the job has come and gone.

Relationships are not the only part of your personal life that can affect your ability to move on. Many people (mostly men) put their health-related problems on a back burner in order to stay first in the race for success. Carl, a manager in a large investment firm, said:

When I was forty-two years old, I had a heart attack and missed three weeks of work. When I got back, everyone in the office treated me differently, like I was too weak or too fragile to handle the fast-paced, competitive nature of our industry. I've worked extra hard to prove I can handle anything and everything they put in front of me. My doctor told me to follow up with him on a regular basis. But if I do, I'm afraid he'll want me to go back in the hospital for testing. I can't afford to have my company know my health is still an issue—especially when they are getting ready to lay some people off. As soon as I know my job is secure, I'll start taking better care of myself and do what I need to do to stay healthy.

Roxanne, a sales trainer, risked another type of security to protect her job:

I knew my marriage was in trouble, and my long hours and extensive travel weren't helping matters. My husband wanted us to go to counseling. Now I have nothing against counseling, but I couldn't afford to pay for it privately, and my insurance claims go through my company. I sure didn't want anyone to know that I couldn't handle my personal problems, or they might decide I couldn't handle problems at work. So I tried to keep the relationship working until I felt more comfortable with the security of my job. My husband and I are separated now, and I hope it's not too late to get the counseling help we need. I still have my job, but I don't know if the sacrifices were worth it.

We were amazed at how many employees put personal problems, including serious health issues, aside because they feared bringing them out in the open could affect their chances of keeping their jobs. If you are going to take charge of your own career and focus on staying employed, you must take care of any problems that affect your personal life. You must do everything in your power to stay healthy in mind, body, and spirit. And you must work hard to keep your personal relationships strong, safe, and supportive. Why is all this so important? If you do lose your job, you will need your health, along with the support and encouragement of family and friends, to give you the strength and ability to explore new options.

Employees must also expect that in the future they may have to take on the responsibility of providing and paying for their own health and life insurance, benefits that have previously been provided by their employer. They also need to be aware that many companies who have offered employee assistance programs, counseling, and substance abuse programs are considering cutting back or eliminating these "extras" as well. Remember, cutting benefits is an expedient way for a company to save money. Therefore, employees need to be proactive and informed about alternative ways to provide the help and insurance they need. Keeping your options open means carefully planning for your financial future and security for yourself and your family in the event they become your sole responsibility.

2. Demonstrate value added

Perhaps you've decided you want to quit your job and move on. Or maybe the company decided for you, and now you're on your own. If you want to stay employed, it's imperative that you be able to demonstrate to a new employer or company that you are vital and essential to their number one goal of making a profit.

It may have been quite a few years since you've had a job interview, and in your haste to find employment you may overlook some very important points. We recommend that you do not go on any interview without first taking the time to do some careful and extensive research into each potential employer. Go to the library, use the Internet, gather information, and talk to people who work for the company you are considering. Who are their customers? How can you help to retain them or bring in new customers? How can you help them increase productivity? These are the questions you must be prepared to answer.

It's also important to know where a company is going in terms of the future. What kind of reputation does it have? Is it respected in the industry? What is its track record for success? What are some future trends that could possibly affect its ability to keep you on as a valuable employee? Remember, the company you are interested in has probably gone through some downsizing in the recent past. Consequently, it must be very selective about hiring new people, since it has specific objectives to meet and is looking for people who can help accomplish those objectives. How can you prove your value to that company?

Take an approach that will set you apart from the rest of the applicants this company will interview. The interviewing process is very different today than in the past. Laws today prevent employers from asking some of the personal questions they were once allowed to ask. Therefore, it is up to you to offer as much information as possible that will encourage them to hire you. The best thing you can do is to use these eight high-performance traits as guidelines. Since these are the qualities employers are looking for, let them know up front that you have exactly what they want.

To do that you must talk about the skills, talents, and abilities you have that will make you a valuable employee. Talk about your positive attitude, and how your energy and enthusiasm can help motivate your colleagues and bring back lost customers. Talk about your ability to communicate assertively and work cooperatively in team settings. Discuss your flexibility and willingness to accept change—and even initiate it when a new idea seems appropriate. Let them know you are a good leader, teacher, and mentor, but can also follow others and learn from them. Make sure they know you are not afraid of hard work and that you can definitely help them increase productivity. And don't forget to mention that you are always in the process of learning more about yourself, your job, your company, and the future of your business.

While honesty is crucial in preparing your résumé, don't forget the importance of creativity. Just as you want to stand out from the crowd at your interview, your résumé should also set you apart and encourage your potential employer to take a second look at your abilities. Is there something unique about your talents and skills that the other people applying for the job might not have? Paulina told us a great success story:

I interviewed with a company I really wanted to work for, but they were very noncommittal. A week later, I got a call from the CEO. He remembered from my résumé that I spoke fluent French. He had two potential investors coming from Paris to tour his plant and they did not speak a word of English. He asked if I would be willing to spend a few hours the next day (a Sunday) to serve as interpreter. Of course, I jumped at this opportunity. The day was a great success. The company got the contract, and three months later, I got the job. The CEO told me I had some important strengths he could really use to help his company expand. And to think I almost decided not to include my French skills as an "extra talent" on my résumé.

Your creativity will really be important in your job search, as Kerri learned:

When my company decided to replace me with someone half my age, it wasn't long before they realized this person had lots of book knowledge, but only half the experience I had. I knew they could not take me back full-time, so I proposed a deal they couldn't refuse. I now work for them, one day a week, as an outside consultant. We are not bound by a full-time contract, and they are still getting the benefit of my knowledge. What about the other four days of the week? No problem! When I saw how well this was working out, I contacted some other companies in our industry, and I have the same arrangement with each of them. It's worked out well for all of us, and I'm still employed full-time.

Your options and opportunities will be greatly increased if you can demonstrate to prospective employers that your abilities will add value to their companies.

3. HAVE A POSITIVE IMPACT ON YOUR SITUATION

To be willing and ready to explore new options, you must also be determined to have a positive impact on your situation and yourself. If you are worried about losing your current job, are presently out of a job, or are going through a transition period between jobs, you may be experiencing a barrage of mixed feelings including anger, anxiety, sadness, bitterness, fear, and apathy. A positive attitude and the determination to move on and discover new opportunities will play a big part in whether or not your undesirable situation can be turned around.

True, this is easier said than done. The very thought of losing one's job, let alone the reality of it, can certainly diminish the optimism of even the most positive person. If you have gone through a downsizing or merger, you may experience feelings of betrayal, loss, and helplessness, believing that "life will never be the same." Or you may be feeling very frustrated and angry, tired of worrying about what will happen next. You're fed up with working for such an unfair company. But nothing seems to be fair in today's job market. Barry, a regional vice president of a large insurance company, told this story:

> I'd been with this company for twenty-seven years, and in all those years I received nothing but excellent evaluations. I was promoted several times, which meant I had to uproot my family, move, and start over. I was now living in a community I really loved, in a position I had worked hard for many years to achieve. Then our division was bought out by another company. I was in competition for my job with one of their guys who had nowhere near the experience I had. It never occurred to me I would not be chosen. But I didn't count on the fact that the acquiring company was more committed to keeping its own employees than to placing the most qualified candidate. Everyone agreed I was the best person for the job, but the acquiring company made the rules. And that sure wasn't fair.

If you believe your situation is unfair, no one will deny your right to be angry and bitter. But the real question is: "Now what are you going to do about it?" Negative emotions are downright debilitating and destructive. You will probably experience some of them as part of the natural process of accepting your situation. But you don't have the time or the luxury to make them a permanent part of your personality if you are truly interested in staying employed. You'll be too busy checking out your other options.

You must take charge of your attitude and literally teach yourself to work through your negative emotions and into more positive and productive ones. Because eliminating or defusing a negative attitude takes work, you must want to feel differently. You must take whatever negative feelings you may have and leave them behind. Drop them. Move on. Your feelings can, and will, direct your actions. Many people tell us, after losing their job, "I'll never be the same" or "I'll never get over this." If that's how you feel, and that's what you keep telling yourself, then you're probably right. This setback could very well be your undoing.

Wayne, who lost his executive vice president position, said:

I don't feel like doing anything. I haven't for months. I loved my job. I was really good at it. I can't believe this happened. I'll never get another job like the one I had. So why bother to try?

And Carla expressed negative feelings:

My family says I'm depressed. Of course I'm depressed! I have a right to be. I had a great job, great income, great benefits— and now they're gone. I'm afraid to start all over with a new company. I don't think I can go through this again.

There is no doubt that Wayne's and Carla's negative feelings will seriously affect their future employability. Like them, many other employees are giving up control of their future, content to play the role of the victim. Perhaps you have had to give up your job, your salary, or your title, but no one can force you to give up control of your life and your future. A job is replaceable. Your determination, attitude, character, and potential are not. No one can take these things away from you unless you give them permission to do so.

If your goal is to stay employed, then you must believe that you will be able to get through difficult situations and move on successfully to other opportunities. Be resolute and determined, think positive thoughts, and engage in behaviors that will have a positive impact upon your career. You must take charge.

Unlike Wayne and Carla, Ray chose to view his situation in a positive way:

I was given one week's notice to leave a job I'd had for eighteen years. My "severance package" is a joke. I had every right to be angry, bitter, and sad, and I gave myself all day Tuesday to experience those feelings. On Wednesday I put the past to rest, opened up the classified ads section of the paper, and called an employment agency. I have bills to pay, and my family is counting on me. I can't afford the luxury of being angry. I need to focus all my energy on getting a job and staying employed.

Your attitude about yourself, your job, and your situation will determine your opportunities for employment in the future. Can you count on a positive attitude to get you through the tough times? If you can't, what are you willing to do about it?

4. EMBRACE CHANGE

Starting a new job can be very stressful because it often requires us to make many adjustments all at once: a new office, new colleagues and co-workers, new rules, new expectations, new people to impress. We're sure you could list many more. Sometimes we must even relocate. In other words, accepting a new job means that we have to make many changes. And we are often resistant to change.

Many people are offered jobs comparable to the ones they had, but don't want to move to a different city or state. Others turn down jobs because the new position would require more education and training. If you have the luxury of turning down several jobs until the right one comes along, this is not a problem. But don't refuse to consider what might be an excellent opportunity because you are afraid to change.

Expanding your horizons by additional education and training can be very rewarding. Consider Theresa's story:

I had worked for the same company for over twenty years, and when I got laid off, I spent some time deciding what I wanted to do with the rest of my life. I had been out of school for many years and was rusty at studying. So I went back to college and took a very intensive paralegal course (the equivalent of three semesters compressed into one). Then I got into graduate school and I'm studying in a field where I can combine my paralegal training and education with my master's in this new field. I first thought my career was over, but now I'm excited about my new beginning.

Janine was willing to take a job with a smaller company for less money and less authority, but she believes the trade-off was well worth it:

When our CPA firm merged with a larger one, downsizing rumors began flying right away. I had been looking for an opportunity to do something a little different instead of working for such a big company. For years I had kept the books for a friend. His small business had grown and he was ready to bring someone on full-time. I told him I was the perfect candidate for the job, since I knew his business as well as he did. I love working with this smaller company, and I'm excited to see how we've grown. I'm making less money, but I have more time for the hobbies and interests I never had time to enjoy. In my old job, I was responsible for twelve people in my area. Now I enjoy the freedom of being responsible for no one else but me.

As Brad pointed out, sometimes a new job brings new responsibilities and makes you aware of skills within yourself that you had never tapped before:

After being downsized out of a Fortune 500 company, I found a good job with a small firm. As an engineer, I was excited about getting out in the field again instead of being stuck behind a desk. After landing my first big contract, I came back to the office to delegate the details to my staff person so I could get back out there and land another project. To my surprise, my boss handed me a laptop and said, "Meet your staff." It took me a while to get used to doing everything myself. Now I'm the delegator and the delegatee! But once I got over my initial reaction of "I'm way too important to do all this detail stuff myself," I found I really do enjoy taking each project from start to finish. It was a big transition, but I knew I had to change my self-perception if I wanted to make this new job work for me.

To stay employed, you cannot be resistant to change. You must be willing to explore all your options, even if that means getting more education and training, acquiring new skills, accepting new responsibilities, and moving to a new location. You can't expect employers to adapt to your individual needs. You must adapt to theirs.

5. WORK HARDER AND SMARTER

If you are between jobs or starting a new job, you must be prepared to work harder than ever. It is, in fact, hard work to:

- Be as positive and productive as possible.
- Concentrate on personal relationships and do what needs to be done to feel safe and supported.
- Keep studying and learning.
- Work effectively with a team.
- Prove to someone that you and your job are necessary to your company.
- Write résumés and letters.
- Network and meet new people.
- Interview, knowing someone is judging and evaluating your appearance, knowledge, skills, and potential.
- Change, leave your comfort zone, and explore all your options.
- Take charge of your career and your future.

Remember, there are only two reasons why people do not live up to their full potential in both their personal and professional lives. They are either unable to do so, or they are unwilling to do so. If you are unable to do what needs to be done, then take the necessary steps now to take charge of your career and your future. If you need help, that is perfectly acceptable. There are companies that can work with you to write a dynamic, eye-catching résumé. Consultants can teach you how to interview assertively and effectively. You can go to school to acquire new skills. Counselors can help you work through your personal problems. It is up to you to overcome the obstacles that prevent you from moving on to the next step in your career.

Perhaps, however, you are perfectly able to accomplish all these things, but you are unwilling to do so. Most people who choose not to take charge and do what is necessary to live their lives to the fullest are often the people who cannot let go of negative emotions. These feelings can literally replace the positive energy you need in order to move ahead. Are your feelings about your situation keeping you from exploring the new and possibly exciting options open to you? If so, learning to look at yourself differently—as someone who has choices rather than someone who feels like a victim—might very well be the hardest job you will ever have. But if you intend to stay employed, you must deal with these issues. Every CEO, manager, human resource director, and employer we interviewed said they wanted to hire and retain people who were enthusiastic and optimistic about themselves and their future.

6. COMMUNICATE OPENLY AND DIRECTLY

If there ever was a time to be able to communicate effectively, this is it. To stay employed, you will have to network, meet and talk to new people, share information, and go on interviews. Everywhere you go, you will meet and make an initial impression on people who could possibly pave the way for new opportunities. People you meet may know someone . . . who knows someone . . . who knows someone else . . . and you have a new lead. An initial conversation often includes the question, usually asked out of curiosity or courtesy: "So, what do you do for a living?" Depending on your current situation, your answer may vary. Perhaps you are employed but feel your job may be in danger. Or you have a job you don't enjoy and you want to explore other options. Or maybe you are unemployed. Whatever your situation, it's important that you have an answer ready which will briefly describe your current job or the kind of job you would like to have.

This can be very difficult for people who find themselves out of work for the first time. In the past, unemployed people were often viewed as lazy, incompetent, or "unable to hold down a steady job." As a result, many people feel self-conscious or embarrassed to tell others they are currently unemployed. But the sometimes narrow stereotype of people who are unemployed is rapidly changing. Today thousands of honest, capable, hardworking, competent, and skilled people are finding themselves unemployed through no fault of their own. "Unemployed" can be a circumstance, not necessarily a measure of someone's ability or character.

If you are unemployed, the first thing you must do is to accept that fact. Next, practice the phrase "I am currently unemployed" until you can say it without embarrassment, guilt, or apology. When he was asked his occupation, Edward answered assertively, "As a result of a downsizing in our hospital, my job as director of marketing was eliminated. I chose not to accept an offer to manage the purchasing department so I could look for another marketing job, which is the field I'm really good in and what I really enjoy." In those two sentences Edward communicated important information about his qualifications, his goals, and his positive attitude.

How do you answer when someone asks what you do? Hopefully not like Cindy, whose response was, "What do I do? Nothing. I just lost my job. I can't believe it. Thirteen years I gave them, and this is how they thank me. I'll never trust another company again. Oh, but I didn't answer your question. I was a manager for a doctor's office. I didn't really like it, but it was a job. I know you work with a lot of hospitals and physicians so if you hear of a job, let me know, okay?"

No, it's not okay. Why would anyone take the risk of recommending Cindy for a job? In a few short sentences she communicated her anger, resentment, and the fact that she did not like her job. When you're looking for a job, every person you meet is a potential lead and you should communicate in a positive and professional way.

To communicate your needs effectively and succinctly, you must think clearly about what you are qualified to do and how you could apply those qualifications to a challenging and rewarding job. Then put that information into two short sentences like Edward did and practice them until you can communicate that information in a positive way. You'll be amazed at how many people will say, "Oh, my brother-in-law works in that business. Let me give you his number" or "I work with a client who might be interested in you. Let me call him for you." New contacts, new possibilities.

Many people looking for employment think that if they have a good résumé and send it to enough people, someone will eventually call and offer them a job, or at least an interview. But finding the right job takes more than that. You have to actively market yourself and your abilities, because many people are competing for the job you want. It's entirely possible that your next lead might appear when you least expect it, so you must be prepared to take advantage of every opportunity to communicate your needs and goals to every person you meet.

7. LOOK FOR LEADERSHIP OPPORTUNITIES

Your ability to take charge of your career future and make good, solid decisions will help determine whether you move successfully through difficult times or remain stuck where you are. Many fine executives, managers, and employees who are known for their outstanding leadership abilities often fail to use those abilities when faced with a potential or real job loss.

These are the leadership qualities that will definitely help you in times of transition and change:

- You must continue to be trustworthy and act with integrity. Avoid the temptation to criticize your previous company, boss, or co-workers. Don't give away your previous employer's secrets because prospective employers will assume you would do the same thing to them. Don't lie about or exaggerate your abilities, skills, salary, or credentials. Someone will discover the truth and your chances of being trusted again are slim to nonexistent.

- You must still strive to achieve and exhibit high levels of excellence. Your résumé and qualifications must stand out from all the rest.

- Your professionalism must be reflected in your attire, appearance, attitude, and communication skills. Prospective employers must quickly realize that they can count on you to do a top-quality job.

- You must have a reputation for making others feel worthwhile and valuable. Prospective employers will certainly check references from your previous employer to assess your leadership qualities and discover how effective you were as a team player.

- You must never stop being a role model. Even if you must continue to work for several weeks after you know your job is over, others are watching how you handle yourself, and it's important to remain professional at all times. As Charles, manager of a branch of a stockbrokerage firm, said:

I was told my job as regional vice president was being eliminated, and I had six weeks to close down the office. I was angry. But I knew I had to be as professional as possible in front of my employees. They were counting on me now more than ever to help them get through this. I brought in career counselors to help them with their résumés and I motivated and inspired them when they were feeling down. I kept my sense of humor and tried to set a positive example. In my heart I know I was an outstanding manager down to the very last moment in that office.

- You must continue to serve others, even if your job is in jeopardy. Working to help others in your company survive change can create great advocates for you in the future. Charles continued:

  One of my former department managers, Evelyn, got a new job with an excellent company right here in my hometown. Evelyn said she was so impressed by the way I handled everything during the downsizing that she told her new company about me and I have an interview next week that looks very promising.

- Service to your community is also a great network builder. Many people have found new jobs through associations they developed in community activities. What about you? Can you work on a telethon to raise money for a worthy cause? Can you get involved in the Chamber of Commerce, Scouts, or your church groups? And what about membership in trade associations to increase your visibility? A record of your community service may set you apart from other job applicants in a prospective employer's eyes.

- You must be able to demonstrate your ability to teach, mentor, and coach. At a time when teamwork is the focus of many companies, prospective employers are looking for people with these skills.

- You must be able to show that you are good at relationship building. Effective teamwork is built upon strong, supportive relationships and prospective employers are looking for people who can build and maintain them.

- You must have a vision for the future. It is vital during times of transition. What is your vision for the future? Perhaps you can get a better picture by answering the following questions:

  1. How would I describe "the perfect job"?
  2. What would I be willing to give up to get this ideal job?

3. What should I be doing differently from what I'm doing now?
4. Where do I see myself in one year . . . three years . . . five years?
5. How will I get there?
6. What are the strengths I will need?
7. What must I do to make my vision a reality?

You must be able to draw on your leadership abilities to motivate yourself to explore new options and opportunities. And remember, prospective employers are looking for people who are willing and able to assume a leadership role—whatever their job level.

8. Commit to lifelong learning

An important part of lifelong learning includes knowing yourself well enough to understand how you react to what is happening in your career. Three different people who were all laid off from the same company shared valuable insights about how they handled the situation:

According to Dave:

I was so angry and so hurt when my boss called me in to tell me I was being laid off. My pride got the best of me and I shouted: "After all I've done for this company! You can't fire me—I quit!" Of course that was a huge mistake, since they didn't have to offer me anything after that—no severance package, no outplacement help, no continuation of my health benefits for even six months. I felt great when I got everything off my chest, but it was not the smartest thing I've ever done. I made a big mistake and I didn't get a second chance.

Compare that with Jeff's response:

I was also angry when my boss called me in and said there was no longer a place for me with the company. But after hearing how Dave had exploded and lost everything, I decided to take a different approach that would serve me better in the long run. I asked to come back the next day and negotiate what I wanted, and my boss agreed. I was amazed at how calm I was only twenty-four hours later, after getting over the initial shock. And I got what I deserved, including stock options and office space to use while I looked for another job. They even agreed to reimburse me for unused sick time and vacation time. All in all, I'm okay, and I'm glad I learned from Dave's mistake.

Leona was proud of how she handled her downsizing experience:

I could see the handwriting on the wall when my supervisor told me my position would be cut from full time to part time. I made an appointment to see our human resource director and went in with a list of negotiating options. He agreed to give me an outstanding letter of recommendation, continue my medical coverage for one year, and I got a good severance package. Most valuable was a connection with a good outplacement firm, which assigned me a counselor who polished up my résumé and put me in touch with other people in my field who may hire me.

What about you? What have you learned about yourself and the way you respond to difficult situations in your professional life? Are you quick to overreact? Do you react passively, refuse to talk about what's happening, and close your eyes to what is going on around you? Or do you face each situation knowing you have the strength, skills, and abilities to survive, no matter what? Although it may be painful, if you can learn to react positively in difficult situations, you will have more options available to you.

One important part of lifelong learning is knowing your strengths and tapping into them to explore all your options. It is crucial to focus on not only the strengths you are using today, but on all the strengths you may not have used to their full potential because they are not—or were not—necessary in your job. What about your strengths at earlier stages of your life? Could they be developed and used to add value to your present job or make you more employable with another company? Your willingness to learn new skills, along with better and smarter ways to do your job, is an important part of your commitment to lifelong learning. Obviously, the more strengths and skills you have, the greater your number of options.

Have you considered becoming an entrepreneur—going into business for yourself—as one of your options? For twenty years Stafford had worked as a supervisor in a manufacturing plant. "But," he said, "I could see that our business was dropping off. Foreign companies could produce our product more quickly and cheaply than we could. I knew it was just a matter of time until my job was over. My wife and I began to look around for other opportunities." That is what keeping your options open is all about—exploring new ideas even before it's necessary.

Stafford continued:

> We built a new house and we needed blinds and shades for every window. When we called companies through the Yellow Pages and began to get estimates, we couldn't believe how expensive they were. We finally ordered them through a discount store and put them up ourselves. They looked great! When our neighbors and friends began asking us to do the same for them, we realized we had the potential to start our own business. We found a supplier, printed our own catalogue, and started out small. Now we work with customers in four states and many builders use our services directly. We go in before a new home is finished and take the measurements. The blinds are made and ready to be installed on the day of the closing, so the new owners can have their privacy, beginning with their first day in their new home. And our prices are the best buy in town for quality shades. My wife has been running the business with my help on the weekends, but we've grown so much it's going to take both of us working full-time to get everything done and keep up with our orders and installations. During the same week I made the decision to quit and take early retirement, my manager called

me in and told me my job was being eliminated. He couldn't believe how well I took the news. Little did he know, I was one step ahead of him.

Starting your own business is something to consider seriously if you are truly keeping all your options open. One thing is certain: if you ever do go into business for yourself, it will be very difficult to work for someone else again. If you decide to take this step, keep the following tips in mind:

1. Remember, your number one goal will be that of any business: to make a profit. In order to do that, you must be able to provide a service or product that is needed by customers. You must also provide them better service or a better product than any of your competitors. Many people begin a business without a good understanding of their potential customer base. For example, a new bagel restaurant with wonderful service and a terrific product may not last if there are three other bagel shops within six blocks.

2. There are plenty of books, tapes, workshops, and conferences especially designed for people who want to become entrepreneurs. Read, attend, and learn as much as possible. Talk to others in the business you want to be a part of. Learn from their mistakes so you won't repeat them. And learn from their successes, too.

3. Never forget that your first job is to run your business. You must be able to perform or oversee the functions of purchasing, marketing, accounting, public relations, and sales. You may love to work with crafts, but that does not mean you have the expertise to open a crafts shop. You must first learn how to run that business. Identify the areas in which you need to learn more, then take a course in business planning, accounting, or any other area that will give you the expertise you currently lack.

4. You will need money to start your own business. Realize that your first profits must go back into the business in order for it to survive.

You must be financially prepared to pay your bills from savings or another source for a while. Don't buy everything at once; but whatever you do buy, make sure it is good quality. Cheap brochures, tacky advertisements, and poor-quality stationery or business cards are examples of first-impression items that will turn customers away immediately. Whatever you do, make sure you do it professionally and do it well.

5. Be creative. Starting your own business is not limited to opening a store where people come in to make purchases and place orders. Technology has allowed us opportunities to work from our homes and still have access to customers everywhere. Many companies that started out as home-based businesses have grown to become million-dollar operations.

Another option is consulting, a field in which business is booming. What skills do you have that others might want, especially if they can contract with you on a part-time basis? After Peggy had been laid off as director of human resources for a major insurance company, she tried to get a similar nine-to-five job with another company to no avail. She was advised to think about contracting her services and expertise in personnel, benefits, compensation, hiring and firing, and employee assistance to several smaller firms that could not afford or did not need a full-time person. Peggy admitted she had never even thought of that. But she printed business cards and letterhead stationery, installed a phone with voice mail and a fax machine, and let people know about the consulting skills she had to offer. Now a year later, she has twelve small companies who use her services from two to ten days a month. She is turning business down. True, she must now pay for her own insurance and overhead, but does she like it? Just listen to Peggy: "This is great. I always wanted to be my own boss. Now I am. I love being able to do things my way. I work harder than ever, but I don't mind because it is my reputation I am building. Losing my job was the best thing that ever happened to me."

Losing a job is always difficult, but it is not a disaster if you keep your options open. And what does keeping your options open really mean? It means not taking your job for granted and assuming it will always be there. It means planning ahead and preparing for possible changes that could affect your job. It means taking charge of your career and not counting on a company to take care of you. It means refusing to be a victim, and instead, taking an active role to ensure that you will always be employable. No one can take better care of you than yourself.

CHAPTER 10

Your Paycheck Is a Thank-You Note

Employees and employers, whatever their line of business, have one thing in common. They want to be respected and valued. One employee told us, "How nice it would be to have a job where management let you know on a consistent basis that you have made a positive difference in the company." This same lack of recognition affects employers as well. One CEO confided:

> I have worked so hard to turn this company around. I have managed to keep our profits up without laying off one person. I provide excellent benefits, and I'm willing to pay for my employees to go to school. I spend a great deal of money on picnics, parties, and celebrations because I want them to enjoy their jobs and feel as though this is a family they can count on. Very few of them have ever said thank you or even seem to appreciate how hard I try to make this a great place to work. On the other hand, if one little thing goes wrong or I have to say no to any of their ideas, some of them threaten to quit. And others won't speak to me.

What does everyone really want? It's very simple: recognition and appreciation. Employees should view every paycheck as their employers' way of saying thank you. But what if employers took this idea one step further and enclosed a real thank-you note with that paycheck? The note might read something like this:

I want to thank you for:

- Contributing to a team with whom I am proud to work. Your dedication, support, and commitment have allowed us to develop the level of trust and cooperation we need to successfully serve our colleagues and our customers.

- Supporting the mission and vision of our organization. You take ownership and pride in the goals we have set and integrate them into your professional life.

- Coming to work with a positive attitude. Your enthusiasm is contagious and you help set the tone for a work environment that is both enjoyable and productive.

- Striving to maintain balance between your personal and professional life so you can give us 100% of your creativity and energy when you are at work.

- Your willingness not only to accept change, but to think creatively and to be a change agent for our team. Your flexibility allows us to stay competitive and productive.

- Communicating openly, honestly, and directly about your needs, concerns, and expectations. I can always count on you to be assertive and forthright.

- Your commitment to working hard. You understand that our increased productivity is necessary for us to stay profitable and to survive and thrive in a competitive world.

- Having the confidence to accept a leadership role when necessary and appropriate. I can count on you to anticipate what needs to be done next without being asked or reminded.

- Taking advantage of the training, education, and resources available to help you do a better job. You understand the importance of up-to-date information, skills, and technology.

- Sharing with me the value you bring to our organization. Your ability to link your job and your performance to our customers' satisfaction makes you a valuable team member.

- Consistently treating your colleagues and customers with dignity and respect. Your attitude, professionalism, and cooperative spirit are all reflected in the way you do your job and your ability to develop and maintain good working relationships.

- Being the kind of person with whom others would CHOOSE to work. You understand that we spend more time here on the job than we do at home, and you have helped create a workplace that is safe, supportive, and positive. I am proud to have you on my team.

Could your employer enclose this thank-you note in your paycheck and mean every word? If not, what changes in your attitude and behavior do you need to make?

Perhaps one of the most unfortunate commentaries on management today is its reluctance, fear, or lack of courage to let employees honestly know where they stand within their companies. You cannot assume that your paycheck is a sign that you have done a good job. Nor can you assume just because you have received a satisfactory performance appraisal that your job is safe or that the evaluation even accurately reflects where you rank among your peers. Employees often mistakenly assume that since no one has reprimanded, counseled, or criticized their work or behavior, they are doing a satisfactory job. This assumption could put their jobs in jeopardy because many managers have a difficult time honestly expressing their concerns and doubts about an employee's performance—even at evaluation time. Therefore, you must make a concerted effort to identify for yourself where you stand within your company. And one good way to do that would be to ask yourself: "Could my employer write this thank-you note to me?"

By the same token, employees should be able to write a thank-you note to their employers, which might read something like this:

Thank you for:

- Creating a team of people with whom I am proud to work. Your leadership has fostered the level of trust and cooperation we need to successfully serve our customers and colleagues.

- Being a positive and optimistic leader. Your enthusiasm about our company and its goals is contagious. You set the tone for a positive and productive work environment where I feel safe, supported, and valued.

- Providing the training, education, and resources I need to provide the quality service our customers have come to expect.

- Sharing the vision and mission of our organization. By helping me understand the future of our industry, you enable me to see where I fit into the big picture.

- Identifying and embracing change. Your flexibility and creativity in meeting these new challenges give me the courage to do the same.

- Communicating openly and honestly with me about your needs, concerns, and expectations. I always know what is expected of me and where I stand among my peers and within our organization.

- Listening to my opinions, even when we may not agree. I always feel comfortable sharing my ideas and concerns with you because you take the time to listen to me.

- Treating me with dignity and respect, and modeling the values our organization represents: integrity, excellence, commitment, quality service, dependability, and fairness. You demand as much from yourself as you expect from others.

- Being a leader I would choose to follow. You understand true leaders do not rely on threats, power, or intimidation but rather on the strength of their character and their ability to earn others' trust and respect. I am proud to be part of your team.

Could you write this thank-you note to your employer and mean every word? Is this how you feel about your company? If not, what might it tell you? If you honestly believe you are not being treated well or compensated fairly, then you must address the problem. If the company you are working for does not provide the training or resources necessary to do your job, fails to communicate openly, or does not appreciate its customers or employees, then begin today to acquire new skills and explore new opportunities and options so that you can position yourself to work somewhere else as soon as possible.

Many employees say that they absolutely hate what they do and where they work. But they have done nothing for years but complain and gripe. Not once have they made the effort to move up, on, or out. Maybe they think all they have to do is stick it out for three (or five or eight) more years before they retire. They'll survive somehow. But will they really survive? They could be fired tomorrow. And is mere survival all you want out of your job? Are you really ready to give up three or five or eight years of your life because you don't want to make the changes necessary to find a more rewarding job? Too many people live life as though it were a dress rehearsal. They say: "Next time I'll do it differently." There is no next time. This is it. You have to start doing things differently now if you want to stay employed.

Most of us would like to believe that our jobs are meaningful and worthwhile. We have a need to make some sort of significant contribution and take pride in our accomplishments. Are you proud of what you do? Do you believe your work, your skills, and your talents are making a worthwhile contribution? Often employees will answer no to these questions because they believe that to do meaningful work one must discover a new vaccine, compose a symphony, or save a life. We believe that there is inherent value in any job done well and with a sense of pride. Meaningful employment does not refer to what your job is, but how you do that job in terms of your commitment to quality service, honesty, dependability, integrity, and treating others with dignity and respect.

How you do your job is also crucial to staying employed. Remember, there are no guarantees in today's job market. But employers are most likely to hire and keep employees who can demonstrate the eight high-performance abilities we have written about here. In other words, your employability is up to you. You and you alone are in charge of your career—and the rest of your life.

Acknowledgments

This book could not have been possible without the employees and employers who willingly shared their stories and concerns with us, and we thank all of them for their open and honest feedback. We especially want to thank our friend, author Michael LeBoeuf, who introduced us to our Simon and Schuster editors Fred Hills and Burton Beals. Fred, Burton, and assistant editor Hilary Black have been excellent teachers and mentors. Thanks also to our agent, Richard Pine.

We appreciate the help and advice that was always available from our colleagues in the National Speakers Association. And last but not least, we thank our families: our husbands, Larry Podesta and Les Gatz, who probably know this book by heart ("Would you read this chapter just one more time and tell me what you think?"), and our children, who kept asking us, "Mom, are you finished with the book yet?" Yes, we are. And our thanks to all of you.

Index

behavior:
  beliefs vs., 56
  see also positive attitude
behind-the-back game-playing, 106
Ben (bookstore chain district manager), 114–15
benefits, 40, 82, 164
Benita (follower), 138
Betsy (shopping mall employee), 90–91
"big stuff," separating "little stuff" from, 27–28
Bill (purchasing agent), 45
bookstores, 114–15
boredom, 76
bosses:
  as advocates, 52
  leaders vs., 129, 130
  use of term, 129
Brad (downsized employee), 171–72
Brady (technology employee), 96
bragging, documentation of accomplishments vs., 48
Brandon (sales manager), 47
Brian (industrial foreman), 21–22
Brian (insurance specialist), 162
burnout, 97
business owners, 83
  becoming, 180–82
  change agents and, 67, 77
  employees' demonstration of value added and, 55, 65

cable television, 142
call waiting, 120
car dealerships, 146
Carl (investment firm manager), 163
Carla (department manager), 111–12
Carla (downsized employee), 169
Carlos (sporting equipment manager), 87
Carnegie, Dale, 142
cellular telephone industry, 136
cellular telephones, 88

CEOs, 83, 146–47, 167, 173, 184
  change agents and, 67–68, 69–70, 73–75, 78, 79
  e-mail and, 121–22
  employee leadership and, 129, 130, 131, 135, 139, 141
  employees' demonstration of value to, 32–33, 34–35, 37, 43, 45, 46, 50
  employees' positive attitude and, 55, 62, 63–64, 65
  expectations of employees in bad times, 27
  honest and open communication and, 101–2, 104, 111–12, 117–18
  and working smarter, harder, faster, better, 84–85
Chad (line supervisor), 85–86
change:
  of attitudes and beliefs, 23–31
  as constant, 145–46
  in education field, 147–48
  embrace and initiation of, 9, 67–80
  keeping options open and, 170–72
  resistance to, 14–15, 71, 73–74, 77, 92–93
  technological, 84, 85–88
change agents, 67
character, 11–12
Charles (stock brokerage manager), 176, 177
charter schools, 148
chemical refineries, 11
childbirth, change compared to, 71
childhood experiences, 20, 21–22
Christen (manager), 118–19
Cindy (downsized employee), 174
Claire (insurance employee), 107
Cliff (retail clothing salesman), 111
clothing industry, retail, 111
Colette (telemarketer), 91
communication, 63, 101–25
  aggressive, 106, 107–9
  assertive, 106–7, 112–13

lawn and garden centers, 98–99
Leadership Is an Art (De Pree),
129–30
leadership opportunities, 126–44
building relationships in, 140–41,
177
customer service and, 128–29
De Pree's definition of, 129–30
effective communication in,
141–42, 177
high achievement and excellence of,
132–33, 176
keeping options open and, 175–78
positive attitude in, 142–43, 177
positive role-modeling in, 136, 176
resiliency in, 143–44
skills evaluation and, 151
teaching as, 138–40, 177
trustworthiness and integrity in,
131–32
validation of others in, 133–35,
176
willingness to serve in, 136–38,
177
LeAnne (sporting goods employee),
38
learning, lifelong, 9, 145–57
changing workplace and, 145–49
keeping options open and, 178–80
mentors and, 155–57
skills identification in, 149–51
updating of skills and, 151–54
leisure time, 98–100
Leona (half-time employee), 179
Lewellyn (customer service employee), 125
listening skills, 116–19
"little stuff," separating "big stuff"
from, 27–28
loyalty, to job, 158–59
Lyndsay (insurance employee), 89–90

magazines, 91–92
management consultants, 116

managers, 173
as advocates, 52
change and, 67, 70, 72, 73, 75–76,
78, 79
confused needs of, 8–9
demonstration of added value and,
32–33, 34, 37, 41, 45, 47, 49,
51–54
e-mail and, 122
employee leadership and, 129, 130,
131, 135, 138
employees' positive attitudes and,
55, 62, 63, 65
honest and open communication
and, 101–2, 104, 107–8,
114–15, 117, 118, 124–25
lifelong learning and, 150–51, 153
mid-level, 11
multiple roles of, 18
reluctance to delegate duties by, 130
manipulation, 106, 107–8
manufacturing companies, 64
Marcia (receptionist), 151–52
Margaux (computer analyst), 61–62
Maria (travel agency employee), 94
Marilyn, 41–42
Mark (bad writer), 124
Mark (medical technician), 108
Mark (purchasing agent), 39
marketing, 35–36, 48–49
marriages, abusive, 20–21
Marriott, Bill, 132
Marsha (packaging plant employee),
92
martyrs, 108–9
Mary (recycling employee), 30
Mayflower, 68
medical equipment companies, 38
medical laboratories, 108
mediocre performance, 83–84
meeting planners, 154
Megan (packaging plant worker), 92
mentoring, 155–57
Meredith (toy company owner), 88
Mickey Mouse, 58

About the Authors

Connie Podesta is an international professional speaker, keynoter, and trainer, and has addressed over a million people throughout the world in all areas: business/industry, health care, and education. She has a B.S. in communications and speech and an M.S. in human relations and counseling. Her experiences as Director of Employee Assistance, Director of Staff Development, educator, business owner, and consultant to some of the top *Fortune* 500 companies have given her a unique insight into the business world today. She lives in Dallas with her husband, and has two grown daughters.

Jean Gatz is a nationally recognized professional speaker and workshop leader. She presents keynotes, workshops, and in-house employee training programs for thousands of people each year in health care, education, business, industry, government, and a wide variety of associations. She holds a B.S. in psychology. Drawing on her diverse background as an office manager, teacher, employment counselor, consultant to business and industry, and owner of her own company, she brings a wealth of knowledge and experience to this book. She and her husband live in Baton Rouge, Louisiana. They have three grown children.

If you would like to reach us:

Connie Podesta
1900 Preston Road, #267-294
Plano, TX 75093
www.conniepodesta.com

Jean Gatz
P.O. Box 40612
Baton Rouge, LA 70835